COSMIC MESSENGERS

COSMIC
MESSENGERS

The Universal Secrets to Unlocking Your Purpose
and Becoming Your Own Life Guide

ELIZABETH PERU

HAY HOUSE

Carlsbad, California • New York City
London • Sydney • New Delhi

First published in the United Kingdom by:
Hay House UK Ltd, Astley House, 33 Notting Hill Gate, London W11 3JQ
Tel: +44 (0)20 3675 2450; Fax: +44 (0)20 3675 2451
www.hayhouse.co.uk

Published in the United States of America by:
Hay House Inc., PO Box 5100, Carlsbad, CA 92018-5100
Tel: (1) 760 431 7695 or (800) 654 5126; Fax: (1) 760 431 6948 or (800) 650 5115
www.hayhouse.com

Published in Australia by:
Hay House Australia Ltd, 18/36 Ralph St, Alexandria NSW 2015
Tel: (61) 2 9669 4299; Fax: (61) 2 9669 4144
www.hayhouse.com.au

Published in India by:
Hay House Publishers India, Muskaan Complex,
Plot No.3, B-2, Vasant Kunj, New Delhi 110 070
Tel: (91) 11 4176 1620; Fax: (91) 11 4176 1630
www.hayhouse.co.in

A catalogue record for this book is available from the British Library.

ISBN: 978-1-78817-064-2

Interior star image: Deltawaves Pty Ltd

Certified Chain of Custody
SUSTAINABLE FORESTRY INITIATIVE
Promoting Sustainable Forestry
www.sfiprogram.org
SFI-01268

SFI label applies to text stock

There have been many souls who have assisted me on my journey.

To my soul family, your support and guidance inspire and direct me.

*To my global community, your love and dedication
to advancing your life, fuel me.*

*And to blue wolf, whose steadfast encouragement
and love enable me to fly.*

CONTENTS

PART II: BECOMING A COSMIC MESSENGER

LIST OF PRACTICES

INTRODUCTION

You are Needed

For millennia – in a myriad of guises and forms – there has only ever been one *you*. The being that you are is a unique blend of experiences and energy that produces a soul who has ample opportunity to rise to greatness.

Yet how many of us actually accept this challenge of personal fulfilment and delve into the mysteries of life in order to find our place within the universe? What would happen if you were to become aware of your true origins? Would knowing where you come from, who you are and why you're here, help you to focus and find a deeper meaning and direction in life? Have you ever considered this?

Would knowing that you were born of the stars, and that you're a natural *Cosmic Messenger*, open up a whole new avenue of discovery for you – one that confuses and confronts as much as it answers and inspires?

This book has been written for enquiring souls: those who hunger for a purpose, a connection to the cosmos and a path that utilizes all of their born-with talents. It's a book that speaks to souls who feel they are here for a higher reason and are ready to contribute their all to the planet.

Are you one of these souls? Are you seeking, searching and desiring to know more, so you can live the life that you know you came here to lead? Welcome, Dear Reader. You are magnificent beyond measure. Your light shines like a beacon throughout the universe, and the potential that lies within you is eternal. You *do* make a difference – just by being you.

Even if you never 'woke up' to who you are, you would still impact on all of us because of your presence in the cosmic dance of life. Yet you have more than just an inkling of who you are and why you're here. Don't you? This is what has drawn us together and aligns our hearts as we speak.

My story

Many years ago, I was perhaps as you are now. At the age of 28 I was disillusioned with the direction my life was taking, and I was looking for my answers in earnest. I spent hours on my own, just diving into my thoughts and hoping I'd receive some clarity on why my life had turned out the way it had. I felt alone, and yet I also sensed that this was where I was meant to be.

Not a day went by that I didn't look for a reason for my past actions and those of the people I loved. I'd created a cycle of self-evaluation that felt necessary. I needed to go in deep if I was ever to rise above my questioning and receive my lightning-bolt moment. Can you relate to this?

Then, during this cycle of deep contemplation, I started to experience something quite strange during my sleeping hours.

Each night, I'd wake between 2 and 3 a.m. and, although I was aware of my body in the bed, I was unable to will myself to move. The strangest sounds seemed to emanate from within my home, like knives slashing and bees buzzing. I could feel what seemed to be every atom in my body vibrating and heaviness on my chest – as if something was trying to get into me. Yet, as I was about to discover, it was actually me who was trying to get out.

One night when my body wouldn't stop buzzing, I asked myself, *Is this good for me?* The energy subsided, but then, as I relaxed back into my bed, a vibration rose up my body until it reached my crown. I felt myself leave my body and travel through a roller-coaster-like tunnel of light and sound. It was the most magnificent cosmic trip, and I just knew I was about to find out something extremely important about the meaning of life.

Suddenly, I arrived in a still and quiet space. It was dark momentarily, and then the most sparkling colours and geometric shapes – like stained glass – began to form before me. I was dazzled by their brilliance; so much so that I snapped back into my body and slowly felt myself *wake up*.

My body felt so heavy in the bed, yet I was excited because I knew I had been somewhere that was *soulful*. I had been out of my body and yet I was still me. While I had been out 'soul travelling', I'd had no concern for my body back in my bed: I was just looking to explore the cosmos and the answers and experiences that awaited me.

That moment changed my life forever. After it, I knew *first-hand* that the soul is eternal, that *the soul is me*, and that we never actually die. It was after many years of these out-of-body events that I had my true *wake-up* experience – on New Year's

Eve 1999 – and that led me to the spiritual path I'm walking today. Indeed, it's also *your* yearning and desire to know your soul's path and cosmic roots that has brought us together. For my experiences and knowledge can help trigger yours.

Each of us tends to be in a hurry, particularly when we awaken to our spiritual reality. A rush of excitement erupts from within when we touch on that seed of truth in our heart. Yet there's a way to accelerate your growth, and your remembrance of why you're here, without stress or fear. It involves understanding and working with the patterns of *cosmic energy*, something I've been doing since 2003 as the author of the weekly online Tip-Off Global Energy Forecast.

The Tip-Off gives my seven-days-ahead interpretations of coming cosmic events, while also providing a weekly life guide. I write intuitively for the entire globe, so you read each day as your own, regardless of where you live. My forecasts are read by people in more than 80 countries worldwide and are known for their uncanny accuracy and their ability to provide support and encouragement during challenging times.

And now, in this book, I share my teachings with you and provide comprehensive, practical guidelines to assist you in your exploration of soul, the cosmos, energy – both your own and that of the planets and stars – and your life path.

How to work with this book

It's my intention that by reading and working with this book, you'll come to understand how energy works and learn ways to awaken your born-with talents, powers and skills, all while increasing your cosmic consciousness. Each chapter reveals one of 13 'Universal Secrets' which, when applied, will enable you to work with the universal forces to master your life.

When we align our own energy with that of the planets and stars, we can utilize their assistance in accelerating our life purpose. We become *Cosmic Messengers* for one another and ourselves. Even if you're unsure of your life purpose at this point, simply tuning in to cosmic energy and extending your presence to meet it will help you along a slipstream of synchronicity and increased manifestation.

I place particular emphasis on bringing information through in a simple and easily understandable way. For I have discovered that the essence of soul is simplicity and that the less convoluted something is, the closer it is to the divine.

In each chapter I've provided opportunities for you to pause and self-reflect, along with practices to help you gain a personal experience of soul, cosmic energy and your destined life path. I advise that you move through the book at your own pace and formulate your answers from within.

- **Part I: Your Being and Life Purpose** will guide you through the processes of life here on Earth, and will assist you in identifying and understanding your purpose for being.

- **Part II: Becoming a Cosmic Messenger** will open you up to cosmic consciousness and your role as a messenger of the divine.

- Parts I and II conclude with two valuable **Reference Guides** that provide detailed information on the physical, spiritual, mental and physical effects of cosmic energy and planetary events.

If, while reading the book, you find anything I say challenging, allow it to pass over you. For what may not resonate with you today, could well do so tomorrow. It's important that your imagination is stirred and that new ideas and pathways are opened within you.

You'll come to discover that once you accept that soul is always leading your life in the direction of your heart's desires, by default you become a Cosmic Messenger. For we need you. We need each of you to rise up and claim your natural birthright and divine inheritance.

Your words have power and your actions deliver your focused intent. Your everyday life can be raised to the level of joyful creation, as you forge a career, relationships, family units, and an environmental, humanitarian and spiritual path that uniquely fits you and benefits the whole.

Our planet is going through a pivotal period of change in which souls are connecting to their cosmic origins and information is being shared as never before. This is your opportunity to live with a foot knowingly within both the spiritual *and* physical dimensions, as a messenger not just upon Earth but *a messenger of the cosmos*.

I invite you to take that leap and make your mark. There's only one being responsible for the evolution of your soul, and that's you. May you find peace, connection, inspiration and enlightenment within these pages. What you do with what you find is up to you…

In love

Elizabeth

PART I

~

Your Being and Life Purpose

CHAPTER 1

Energy and You

As we set out on our foray into the cosmos and explore the path of accelerating the purpose of our soul, it's pertinent that we look first at energy – that delectable source of 'all knowing' that seems to shift and change constantly.

Energy is the lifeblood of the universe – it's a force that we're made of and work with on a daily basis. Are you privy to the nuances of energy, and if so, how can you be at one with energy to utilize it to your full advantage?

What is energy?

Energy is both cosmic (or universal) and internal in nature, meaning it originates from the source of all being and is unlimited in its scope and application. We could say that energy is an invisible pulse, an almost untouchable and yet tangible force that is the origin and also the carrier of our thoughts, ideas, dreams and actions.

While still at its centre, energy produces a wave of moving desire – a wave that we can tune in to and flow with, as and when we choose. Imagine there's an invisible life stream, or essence, that gives rise to all forms of life – etheric, material or otherwise. Rather than being something we need to muster, energy is always at our disposal and is the fuel that powers our life.

An interesting aspect of energy is that it shapes to your desires. So if you're tired in body or mind, you may feel that you have little energy to use. Likewise, if you're feeling vibrant and engaged you may also feel energetic and ready for action.

Yet the energy source you're tapping into is unchanging and always available as a steady resource. It's your desire – your intent – that decides how you'll use the energy you're a part of to your advantage. Every cell in your body is born of energy. Soul is energy. Flesh is energy. Rocks are energy. Planets are energy. All is energy – simply pulsing, moving and being utilized at varying rates.

Each of us has an 'energy body' that is created by layers of subtle energy generated by the physical body's endocrine system. Subtle energy is invisible, yet you can sense it via your feelings. It's your will, your desire – your innermost core – that decides how you'll utilize and interact with energy: the very fabric of which you're made. Understand?

Connecting with energy

Right now, close your eyes and imagine that at the centre of your being is a quiet pulse.

This inner pulse is cosmic in nature. Place your hands over your heart and see if you can tune in and feel it. It's your source and the intelligence that's directing your life. Your inner pulse is pure energy, and you're the director of that energy. When you consciously tune in to it in this way, you're making an express connection with your higher being – with soul. You're also making a direct connection with the cosmos.

Your inner pulse is the being and the one who motivates, decides, directs and experiences your life. This pulse is *you*.

Sensing energy

Even though energy may seem invisible and intangible, it can be experienced in a tangible way. Try this: rub your hands together briskly and then slowly move them apart. Can you feel a buffer between your hands, like an invisible ball?

Play with the energy and move your hands towards and away from each other. Notice how far you can stretch and contract the energy. How does the energy feel? Is it warm, tingly or cool? We all sense energy differently, so there are no definitive answers for what you should be experiencing.

Mindful awareness

Another way to sense energy is to expand your *mindful awareness*. To do this, close your eyes and imagine that your senses can extend for hundreds or thousands of metres around you. It can help to start this focus from your centre (around your heart) and then feel your energy expand and travel outwards.

As you do this, notice how your body starts to respond. Are you picking up any messages? Is the energy cool or hot? Is there a sharpness or softness to what you're feeling? Are you excited at your ability to explore so effortlessly?

As you extend your energy outwards, are you picking up on a particular feeling or sensation? Are you sensing the general feedback, out in the atmosphere? Does it feel positive or negative to you? If you were to write about the energy you're experiencing, what would you say?

Being able to interpret, or read, energy in this way is a skill you can learn through applied practice. It's a valuable tool you can utilize in your everyday life. Chapter 9 goes into further detail about how to read energy and sense the 'energy field', or aura, that extends beyond your body.

Picking up on the energy coming your way, by extending yourself to meet it, means you're prepared and ready for all that the cosmos delivers. Once you start to become aware of the energy that is available to you, all manner of desires can be achieved easily, as you work with the current and upcoming energetic ebbs and flows.

∗ PRACTICE ∗
Experience energy in your body

The following exercise will help you connect with and come to know your own energy flow. You'll also be introduced to the flow of cosmic energy and its messages for you.

1. To begin, find a place where you won't be disturbed and make yourself comfortable. It's best to stand or sit straight, with your arms and legs uncrossed.

2. Close your eyes and move your awareness into each part of your body, from the feet up. Breathe in through the

nose and out through the mouth, relaxing your muscles and releasing any tightness or tension as you work your way up your body. When you feel quite loose and open (this should only take a couple of minutes), you're ready to begin.

3. Start to take note of the energy that you're currently emitting. Are you focused purely on thinking and therefore tapping into the *mental state* of energy? Are you focused on your emotions and therefore tapping into the *feeling state* of energy? Or are you focused on your body and the *physical state* of energy?

4. You can even ask soul which state of energy you're tuned in to. Listen as a message arises, perhaps sounding like a quiet voice from within. Once you have an idea of how well and quickly you respond to and pick up on energy, ask yourself, *What is the current cosmic energy telling me?* Take your time with this and have a notebook handy to write down the messages you receive.

When we make the effort to consciously connect with energy – to speak with it and most importantly, interact with it *knowingly* – we're well on our way to becoming Cosmic Messengers who'll accelerate not only our own life paths, but those of others, too.

Dimensions

As part of our discussion of energy, it's important to look at dimensions, which are the spatial areas through which we experience life.

Before we can create something physically, we first need to engage our imagination: we need to think about and then start 'actioning' our ideas. There's a process for bringing our ideas into form, but perhaps we don't stop to consider the chain of events that occurs in order for us to manifest our desires into the physical dimension.

In this chapter we'll explore the invisible, or spiritual dimension and the visible, or physical dimension, and in so doing, contact our original universal and cosmic nature.

Universal Secret 1:
'Reality is self-created.'

This is the first of our *13 Universal Secrets* – each one of us uses our imagination in order to build up a picture of what it is we *choose* to experience. This is the key to understanding where your true power lies. For indeed, how you see the world around you (the *physical* world) and how it treats you, are directly related to how deeply connected you are to the (*non-physical*) world within you.

When I say *within you*, I refer to a space that exists beyond the body. Close your eyes and notice if you experience a feeling of *going within*. What is happening inside your body? Do you get a sensation that you're *observing* yourself?

If you're just a physical being, how can it be that you're *observing* your physical body, while simultaneously *being a part of* your physical body? Does this imply you're in two places at once? Yes, indeed it does, for we are *multidimensional* beings who are able to travel via the conduit of mind, as we will.

The universal and individual mind

Mind is everywhere: it's an energy field within which we create. There's the *universal mind* and there's your *individual mind*. It's from the universal mind (or source) that we're thought into being as individual souls. Mind or source is your creator and also the giver of all the ingredients that you'll ever need to explore the cosmic universe and create experiences, as you desire.

As a soul, you're a part of the universal mind and you also form an individual mind, based on the experiences that you create in your lifetimes here on Earth or elsewhere. Have you ever wondered why you're attracted to particular historical periods, or are drawn to the future? Do you have a love or natural skill for something that you've never consciously learned during this lifetime? In later chapters we'll look at past and future lives and the experiences that we record upon our soul.

The invisible, or spiritual dimension

Our source, or home base, of soul is the invisible, or spiritual dimension. When we talk of this dimension, we're doing so in relation to the visible, or physical dimension (*see below*), for the spiritual dimension is simply what's *invisible* to our physical senses.

Yet what's invisible to us physically is actually natural to us on a soul level: even though soul may seem invisible in your daily life, there's no denying that soul is there every time you close your eyes or have your heart pierced by an act of love or sadness.

The potency of soul permeates through dimensions. So let's begin to consider that different dimensions do exist and that we can access them with heightened awareness. There are different worlds (dimensions) of experience that we can choose to move in and out of at will.

The more open you are to other dimensions, the easier it is to gain conscious access to them. I say 'conscious' because we're often accessing other dimensions without being aware of it, during sleep for example. If you have a closed mind, it's more difficult for you to consciously travel beyond your body or beyond the physical. It takes practice to be aware of dimensional differences.

Opening up to other dimensions

So, how do we open up to other dimensions? Firstly, by being curious about the true source of who we are and the nature of the cosmic universe. There are many paths that can lead us to the invisible dimension, and once they're experienced, our physical reality can seem quite a flat and limited realm.

Perhaps you've sensed spirit move past you, or heard a voice call out of nowhere? Maybe you've seen sparks of light from the corner of your eye but brushed the experience off, thinking that you're tired or need glasses? Perhaps you've tried meditation for the first time and sensed yourself in subtle or energetic form? By this, I mean have you felt your invisible presence shimmering when in the altered state that meditation delivers?

For the invisible dimension can also be called the spiritual dimension. Spirit is deemed to be that which is the essence of the physical. If someone or something has spirit they have a noticeable connection to a source running deep within them. Therefore, that which is spiritual is the home (or source) of that which is spirit.

We're born of the spiritual dimension, and we never actually leave it. It's from this dimension that we extend our ideas forward and decide to experience the physical dimension. Upon our death, it's the spiritual dimension that soul expands back into.

Experiencing dimensions concurrently

Now consider that as a soul you don't need to leave the spiritual dimension in order to enter the physical dimension. Consider that you're experiencing both dimensions concurrently. You have a foot in both worlds and are a multidimensional cosmic traveller.

How can you know this? Well, have you ever experienced déjà vu? It's a sense of knowing exactly what comes next because you have either witnessed it or lived it already. Have you ever thought of someone and then they contacted you? Has something materialized in front of you, that only *you* saw? Have you ever sensed spirit or made contact with those who've passed or with beings that aren't in physical form?

As we move further into our exploration of the soul, the cosmos and our reason for being, we'll delve deeper into the questions now arising within you. For now, I suggest that you write down your thoughts and your musings on the invisible, or spiritual dimension. Allow your own soul wisdom to rise and guide you to your answers within.

The visible, or physical, dimension

The visible, or physical, dimension is home to our physical body and human life. This is what we often refer to as *our life* in the physical dimension that we inhabit. You have an awareness that you were born; an awareness of which sex you are, of your nationality, of your skin colour, your size, your likes and dislikes, your language, your family and friends, your dreams and desires. And you also have an awareness that one day you'll die.

Time is also something that we're only too aware of in the physical dimension. Yet the transformation of our conscious awareness back into the spiritual dimension after we pass from the physical is something that eludes most of us.

Take a moment now to consider your thoughts on what will happen to you after you die. Do you have a clear vision of the process of leaving your human body, or are you unsure of what will happen? Each one of us needs to decide what (if anything) lies beyond the physical dimension. I trust that by reading this book you'll gain a deeper understanding of your soulful possibilities and the pure potential you emit as a spiritual traveller.

An original idea

Perhaps you'll gain the insight that everything you can see, touch, smell, hear or taste in your physical life began as an *idea* in the spiritual dimension of mind? The physical dimension is born of the spiritual dimension. In order to exist here in the physical, someone or something had to imagine it into being. You imagined your physical body as a soul in the spiritual dimension. Just as animals, plants and minerals all have a consciousness and a will to create life, we all imagine ourselves into being.

Your past experiences (recorded on the energetic fabric of your soul) determined what you would look like, your health, your disposition and your longevity. It may seem that the physical processes of your parents' bodies formed you, yet you decided whom your parents would be, just as they decided that you would be their child.

There's a deeper spiritual reason behind everything that takes place in the physical world. Everything that happens here is the result of an idea that was triggered in the invisible dimension. So while we can try and *fix* issues here on Earth, we often have to go back to the source of what created the issue to begin with. The more we understand the invisible dimension, the more reverence we hold for the physical space that we inhabit.

Thoughts create the physical

If you can accept that every thought you're having is creating and moulding your daily physical reality, you can begin to imagine how empowered you could become. Why? Well, you get to choose what you experience here, based on what you focus on.

If you're constantly having negative or fearful thoughts, then this is the exact physical reality you'll create and experience. If you focus on being positive and bringing through uplifting and inspiring thoughts, then this is the reality you'll create for yourself. One way creates pain and the other, freedom and joy. All choice is with you. Indeed, it takes work on your part to maintain a healthy attitude to your physical life, particularly when you hear about negative world events and see and read media reports that constantly focus on the worst aspects of humanity.

In my experience, it becomes easier to focus on your positives, the more you study the spiritual dimension. As you look for evidence (in your physical life) of how spirit manifests through you, you'll naturally be inclined to feel optimistic about what you're creating each day.

Closing your eyes and going within

When we close our eyes, something magical happens. Instantly the focus is off our physical surroundings and we open up to a dark space where we hover and wait, with a sense that we can attract limitless possibilities.

If you keep your eyes closed for long enough, you'll discover that what you first perceived as darkness now becomes light – full of shapes, visions and images that are so vivid they surpass anything you've ever experienced in the physical dimension.

Closing your eyes and going within is a term you may have heard before. But where is this *within* that we supposedly go to? Perhaps it implies there's an *out there*, as well as an *in here*, which is perfectly plausible. It also infers that when we close our eyes, we're transported within. Within is a space *inside* the body and yet *beyond* the body, all at once. It's a sacred space and one that only you can infiltrate.

When we go within we shut off the outside world and make intimate conversation with the cosmic and the divine. That space within can be considered your inner temple, the place you visit in order to refresh, rewind and receive answers to your outer confusion. When we go within we naturally bring harmony and balance to our physical life. For when we do so, we consciously connect with the invisible, or spiritual dimension.

Connecting within via meditation

There's perhaps no simpler way to connect within, and with the spiritual dimension, than through the practice of meditation. I've come to know meditation as my time to connect with soul and receive the answers that only I can deliver to myself. I trust that you may discover this too. When we meditate we show our trust in our connection with the invisible dimension and our cosmic reality.

Meditation is simple and natural; it's nothing to be scared of. It will make you more productive and sharp, particularly if you're constantly busy and on the go. It doesn't need to be a long, drawn-out process or a convoluted one, for that matter. Even as little as three minutes of meditation a day can instantly reconnect you with the spiritual dimension, making your experience of your physical life all the more meaningful and fulfilling.

You can meditate anywhere and at any time, and no equipment is required. You just need to make an effort to do so. Once you begin to practise meditation on a regular basis, you'll wonder why you never did so before. It'll give you a deeper appreciation for the interconnectedness of life, as you begin to expand your energy field and consciousness to meet and commune with that of the cosmos.

✸ PRACTICE ✸
A way to connect and centre before meditation

Begin your meditation with this easy three-step process; throughout, you'll be breathing in through the nose and out through the mouth.

1. Close your eyes and focus on your feet. Imagine that you can breathe through the soles of your feet. Take a deep breath in, up through your feet. Allow the breath to rise up your body and to leave through your crown. Repeat this three times. Feel yourself connect with the energy of below, the Earth flow.

2. Now in the opposite direction, focus on your crown. Imagine that you can breathe in through your crown. Take a deep breath in, through the top of your head, and carry that breath down your body and out through the soles of your feet. Repeat this three times. Feel yourself connect with the energy of above, the cosmic flow.

3. Now with this dual energy flow of above and below moving through you, focus on your heart, what I call your *soul chamber*. Place your hands over your heart, right over left. Or place your hands in front of your heart in prayer position, which brings consciousness into wholeness.

    Breathe in and out of the heart space three times. Feel the energy of peace and love permeate your entire body and energy field. When complete, open your eyes and feel the connection. Or you can continue with the meditation below.

I suggest that you perform the following simple meditation at least once a day and build up to longer periods as you wish. Consciously connecting with the spiritual dimension through meditation will expand your awareness of other realms and remind you that soul truly is the being driving your human life.

✳ PRACTICE ✳
Simple meditation

Sit, lie or stand and then close your eyes. (Closing your eyes instantly takes your focus from the visible to the invisible dimension. You're there in an instant.)

- Start to use your ears to listen to the *sounds* all around you. Focus on those sounds – this will give your busy personality something to do. If you have trouble with physical hearing, simply hold the intention for your spiritual hearing to kick in.

- See how far out you can listen: push your hearing out of the building you're in. Take your hearing out into space, if you can. What happens? What do you hear? You can also place your hands over your heart or belly and just focus there.

- You're not trying to do anything during meditation, other than slow down your thinking and let your natural energy rhythm take over.

The length of time you stay focused in this way is up to you. If you can do it for at least three minutes at a time to begin with, your personality will start to realize that this is a practice to take note of.

Guided meditation

After I first 'woke up', one of the spiritual practices I was introduced to and enjoyed the most (and still do) was guided meditation. I find that guided meditation is an ideal doorway through which to experience the spiritual dimension, while being conscious in our human body.

Perhaps you're already experienced at meditation and do not wish to be guided, preferring instead to allow soul to take you where you need to be? This is a beautiful experience and one that I love too. However, when I started out, I found that being guided by someone was so helpful, particularly for building my confidence when travelling through dimensions.

You can visit my website, where I have created a library of guided meditations that will connect you with the voice of your soul, as you learn about your life purpose and expand your cosmic consciousness: https://www.elizabethperu.com

It took many months of weekly meditation practice for me to be able to sense colours, sounds or even vivid images in my mind. So go slowly with your process and sink into each step as you find your way back home to soul and the dimension of spirit and the cosmos all around you.

CHAPTER 2

The Soul and the Personality

In Chapter 1, we opened up a doorway of knowing into other dimensions and explored the myriad of opportunities available to us as spiritual beings that are a part of the cosmic universe.

In understanding ourselves as Cosmic Messengers, it's important to contemplate the difference in consciousness between the heart and the head. So let's go a little deeper and look into the very essence of who we are, and how consciousness operates in our physical life.

The soul and the heart

When I first began what I called *soul mentoring* with individuals, I spent many hours on my own, in deep contemplation about life. I asked myself: *What are my burning questions about our human life, and what role does the soul play?*

I figured that my questions would be similar to those of others, and so I was excited to see what my soul would tell me about the nature of how we're formed and how we express ourselves here on Earth.

After weeks of self-enquiry, it eventually came down to *one important question* that needed an answer. This one question seemed so simple, and I was quietly excited that if I could unlock its secret, not only would my life purpose open up, but others' would too.

So, are you wondering what that one question was? Perhaps when you hear it, you'll agree that it focuses on something that we tend to struggle with on a daily basis. For as we live in this physical dimension, we still need to be conscious of our cosmic origins in the spiritual dimension. I won't hold you in suspense any longer. My question was…

'How do I know if it's my head or my heart talking to me?'

That was it. Simple at its core and yet requiring an explanation that I felt could be complex and yet liberating all at once. And so I share with you what (my) soul told me about the heart and the head. This information may be new to you. It may take you a while to absorb it, so go at your own pace. What may at first seem simplistic can actually be the essence of spiritual sophistication.

Your heart

Have you ever pleaded with someone? Have you tried to get your point across with a sincere and heartfelt yearning? If so, consider what part of your body you automatically touch when you want someone to *see you and to hear you*? Where in your human body do you go to when you want someone to connect with the *real you*? Is it your heart or is it your head?

Try it now. Imagine you have the opportunity to achieve a lifelong goal. The universe is listening and is ready to deliver. You just need to express your desire in such a way that it shows your deep longing.

Start talking out loud to the universe and explain why you deserve your desire to come about. Notice which part of your body your hands touch, especially if you say 'please'. Are your hands near or over your heart? Do you at any stage touch your head?

I'm willing to guess that your hands went to your heart at some point. Perhaps the only time we touch our head when expressing our truth is when we're frustrated or in disbelief. Have you ever knocked the base of your palm against your forehead when you've felt you've let yourself down in some way?

Why is it that when we focus on expressing our innermost desires we're drawn to our centre and to our heart, rather than to our brain and our head? If the head is so important in driving our life ahead, then why is it often forgotten, especially in moments of sheer heartfelt feeling and emotion?

Your soul chamber

I put it to you that your heart is the container and emanator of soul in your human body. Your heart is the *soul chamber*. It's where you can access the library of your life books, and it's the physical representation of your eternal being.

The heart pumps life force and blood throughout the body. If your heart stops pulsing, your body will cease to exist. If your brain stops functioning, however, you can still live, as long as your heart continues on. The heart is perhaps the most important organ in your body; it's the first organ to develop in a foetus and with good reason.

Your heart thinks with a different intelligence to the thoughts of the head. Your heart has the cellular capacity to remember and is programmable by the invisible energy (soul) that inhabits it. Heart is where the home is and home is where the heart is.

Place your hands over your heart now and close your eyes. What do you feel? Do you go all warm and fuzzy? Is there a tingling throughout your body? Can you feel the energy of love, a presence? Perhaps a tear forms? What happens if you say 'hello' while connecting with your heart?

Our language and symbolism also speak of the importance of the heart, and in particular of the connection between love, home, the heart and soul. Consider how many phrases we automatically use that connect the heart and soul. How often do you draw a heart to express love? Hearts are seen as the universal representation of love. Now if love can be found within the heart and if soul can be found within the heart, are love and soul one and the same energy?

Your soul

Soul can be expressed as an individualized spark of the divine. As you learned in the last chapter, soul's home base is the spiritual, or invisible (to the physical) dimension. Soul is made of the eternal spirit and can morph and change form at will. Soul is a traveller and yearns to explore its universal home. But how does soul come to be?

Just imagine that there's a great central force at the core of the universe. This core is spirit and it's our mother and father energy as one. Soul is created in (and from) a space of unity. This core-unified energy replicates itself for the sake of creation and each replica is a unique spark of the one unified soul.

Each replica can be called an *individual soul*. Soul is you. Once you're created or born into spirit, you have growing and learning to do, much as you do in your human life. Consider this: you're a much more complex, multidimensional being than just your physical persona.

Soul and unity

There are infinite dimensions through which soul can travel and learn. Soul is curious in nature and created from a source of oneness. Just consider that your true nature is inclusive of all. Your true nature is not split in two, as the physical dimension is. Your true nature knows only unity.

So why would a soul that's made of a unified energy wish to come to Earth and incarnate as a human to experience what we call duality? Well, think about it. Do you ever get bored? Once you know something inside out and experience it day after day, are you then ready for a challenge and desire to try something new?

Just look at children playing with toys. When they want to know how something works, they pull it apart and try to put it back together again. Have you ever noticed this? Rarely do they get it right on the first go. It takes practice to know how to create and recreate something in a flowing and functional form. We can't just imitate and try to make something fit. Soul is the same.

Souls love new experiences, for the more that souls learn the more they can emulate their source of spirit. Often, the best way to learn is to be challenged. Hence, souls see it as an important (and honoured) role to come to Earth and experience creation and destruction through human lifetimes.

Souls come here to understand how *unity works* – by pulling it apart, seeing what makes each part tick and then trying to put it all back together again in a harmonious way. Sometimes we succeed; many times we need to try again. Earth is a physical dimension of opposite energies. There are two parts that make up each distinct whole: the light and the dark, the masculine and the feminine, the above and the below.

A spiritual *and* human being

And so you're in this human body, where you're a spiritual being at the same time that you're experiencing a human or physical existence. It was your decision to be here. Your life is an incredible opportunity that you desired and brought into form. The human body is an exacting vehicle through which a soul experiences physicality.

At conception there's a single egg and a single sperm – the feminine and the masculine, meeting and desiring to work together to form life. Upon agreement, the two become one and a single cell develops. This unified cell lasts for just over a day, before it splits and the process of division or duality occurs and continues throughout our human lifetime.

Hence our ups and downs, our ins and outs and our ever-present struggle to come into unity *are* real. We're living in a divided world yet our true nature (soul) is undivided. It's no wonder that so many people get caught up in the physical world and only ever catch glimpses of soul and the spiritual dimension. It takes conscious work and effort on our part to experience duality as an observer and not become seduced by the headiness and forgetfulness of the human experience.

Your human body consists of many twos: two arms, two legs, two hands, two eyes, two ears, two feet, two lungs, two kidneys, two hemispheres of the brain. But only one heart, although the heart does contain four parts. The heart is the place in your human body where soul feels most at home, and it's what I've come to know as the physical location of the greatest concentration of soul in our human body.

If you wish to connect with soul in your physical body it's ideal to place both of your hands over your heart. Closing your eyes can help to shut out the physical world and more easily open up the unified spiritual field of awareness.

A world of divided experiences

Now when I mention *you* and *soul* in the same sentence, you may be wondering *Who am I? Am I me? Or am I soul?* Well, you're both and at the same time you're also one. As I said, Earth is a physical world of divided experiences. Everything here is polarized and mirrors one another. There's a North and South Pole, an up and a down, a black and a white, a Sun and a Moon.

When we combine energies that are opposites we experience unity. This is why we often attract people who are opposite to us, so that we can experience unity through one another. Of course you're already unified within, yet it can take many years and even many lifetimes of physical experiences to awaken to this knowing.

Soul and you are one and the same being. Yet you have a heart and a head. Your consciousness (your awareness of being) operates within both these centres of your body. So, getting back to my original question – 'How do I know if it's my head or my heart talking to me? – well, I've already gone some way in explaining this.

Consciousness operates between your heart and your head. *There's only one soul, which is you.* In your human body *you* or *soul* is most easily accessed via the heart. However, Earth being a divided reality of physical experiences gives us the impression that everything is split in two.

So, just imagine that soul is given a physical expression, a persona through which you'll interact with the world around you. When you open up to this, what now enters is your *personality*.

The personality and the head

Just as we have a heart to feel and think with, we also have a brain with which to think and interact with the world around us. Our brain is a complex organ, much more complex than the heart. And therein lies an important point: *complexity does not mean superiority, just as simplicity does not mean inferiority.* In fact, quite the opposite can be true.

That which is simple is often the more highly advanced and sophisticated. When we consider that the true nature of soul is unity, it's hard to imagine living a human life with the heart energy leading. After all, we have bills to pay, work to perform, families to be responsible for, our health to consider, relationships to test us… the list goes on.

There are so many physical challenges that a soul may find it impossible to comprehend. So what do we do for ourselves in order to cope with the dense and sometimes fierce nature of the physical world? Why, we create for ourselves a personality. We create a *gatekeeper to the soul*: an energy that is our spokesperson and representative here on Earth.

The gatekeeper to the soul

Many people know the human personality as *the ego*. All of those years ago, when I was asking soul about the nature of the head and the heart, I earnestly wanted a name for our outer expression that wasn't associated with the term *ego*. Why? Well, for so many of us, the word 'ego' has negative connotations, and I felt that our outer expression should be loved, not maligned.

So soul said very simply to me, *You have a personality. It's your personality that gets you through your human life.* When I heard this, my spine straightened and a flush of excitement shot through me. Whenever this happens to me, I know that I've touched upon my truth. Perhaps you're the same? I liked the word *personality* – it was heartwarming and at my core I felt that it resonated with love.

Personality is the human aspect of your consciousness. Just as the fertilized egg splits into two cells and so on after conception, so too does soul form a human identity, somewhat like a twin. Your personality operates in and around the brain and is associated with the head. The realm of the personality is the physical dimension, whereas the realm of soul is the spiritual dimension. We need recognition of both, and to understand how they interrelate, in order to effectively navigate human life.

Your personality is an aspect of your soul. Your personality is not to be dulled down or killed off, but instead nurtured, encouraged and loved. You can think of your personality as a child that needs training and discipline to perform at his or her best.

When it's disconnected from soul, the personality will go off on its own tangent, and indeed this happens for most people until they wake up to the spiritual reality of their existence. It's not wrong or bad that it takes many years (and perhaps many hard-learned lessons along the way) to stop and look for a deeper meaning to our existence. It's simply part of the journey of life that we do this. It's a necessary part, too.

The personality wants and the soul needs

Personality, being directly linked to your human life, is focused on the physical aspects of life and what may seem like necessities for our flourishing survival. Therefore, it's our personality that projects wants and it's soul that creates desires or needs. Desire is born of the heart and has love behind it.

Needs and desires are essential to our existence, whereas wants are *nice to haves* that are also necessary for our growth. It's important to strike a fair balance between needs and wants, soul and personality in our everyday life. This is what brings us into harmony (unity from the division) and a peaceful, fulfilling and contented existence.

The personality emanating from and around the brain is linked to our nervous system, eyes and physical senses. It can be overly concerned with visuals, and with physical appearances in particular. The personality also forms judgements easily, as it strives to do what is best for soul.

For indeed, personality is working for soul and is looking to do the best by us. Your personality wouldn't exist without soul creating it. So how does that make you feel? Is it a relief to know that your personality is an essential part of your soul makeup? Let's now look at how personality and soul, head and heart, work together as a team to accelerate your life and purpose.

Universal Secret 2:
'The heart and the head work as a team.'

The second of our Universal Secrets is that there's teamwork between the heart and the head. The personality can be thought of as your human expression of soul. It's formed by the myriad of experiences you've had in this lifetime and others, whether on Earth or elsewhere in this multidimensional, cosmic universe.

All experiences are recorded upon the fabric of soul (upon our very being), whether they're positive or negative. Therefore, you have a rich resource of wisdom to draw on in your daily life, just by tapping into your soul.

Now to do this and have your personality realize that *soul* is its creator, is a big step. Why not tell yourself now that your personality is divine, for it's the creation of soul? Doesn't that make you love *all* of you? Your heart and your head? Both are needed in order to carry out a successful life journey.

If we're either all in our head or all in our heart, we'll miss out on 50 per cent of life. It's our soul and personality, heart and head, working together as a team – conscious and supportive of one another – that brings about fulfilment and an acceleration of our life purpose.

Heart talk

So, how do you get your head to talk to your heart? Let's begin by saying there's an inner voice that's being generated by your consciousness. When you talk to yourself, where do you think that voice comes from? That inner voice is you. Mostly it's the voice of personality, looking for answers. For the personality is a questioner. Its role is to look after your human body and deliver the messages of soul in your human lifetime.

The personality speaks for the soul and also protects and defends it and your physicality. This is why I call the personality a gatekeeper to the soul. Now most of the time, your personality is out on its own, doing its thing in the best way it knows. Growing up, no one teaches us that we have a personality that takes direction from the soul. If we talk to ourselves or have imaginary friends we're looked upon as being silly or crazy, yet this sort of behaviour is exactly what connects you to soul.

Too often we're brought up to believe that our personality is the sum total of who we are, without any regard for the fact that the soul *creates* that personality. However, perhaps now you're beginning to think differently. Yes?

For soul is in direct alignment with the spiritual dimension and never actually leaves this space, even in your human lifetime, whereas your personality is focused on the physical dimension, for this is where it needs to be to help soul fulfil your purpose in life.

And one more thing. When you pass from this human life you *do* take your personality with you. Personality integrates back into soul and unity, for the personality is an essential aspect of the whole being that we are. It's why souls that come through in mediumship readings (after they've passed) often talk and act just as they did when they were here on Earth. The personality is a part of the soul.

✦ PRACTICE ✦
Align your heart and head and make conversation with soul

Many years ago I taught myself the following very simple technique to drop my head to my heart and have my personality make conversation with my soul. When you perform this on a regular basis you'll find that absolutely any question you have, about *anything*, can be answered by soul.

1. To begin, write down a list of questions that you would like answered. These can be on any topic. You might want to number them or arrange them under headings such as Health, Relationships, Career, Spirituality, Family, Money, etc. Have a pen and paper ready, or something else with which to record soul's response.

2. Now place your questions in front of you. Look at your first question, then close your eyes and place your hands over your heart, right over left. Imagine that all of the

31

energy in your head is dropping down into the chamber of your heart.

Feel your entire presence pulsating under your hands, and when you're ready, ask your first question. I suggest that you ask it silently within. Speak directly into your heart, and then wait.

3. Soul speaks in simple language, much as a child does. Your answers will likely come through in one- or two-word sentences. For example, you may hear the word 'love', or 'yes'.

4. If you need further clarification on your answers, ask for it. Keep asking until the personality feels satisfied with the response received. You'll know when this happens because you'll feel silent within and at peace.

5. Write down your answers and then make sure *you act on soul's advice.*

When you take your own advice and run with it, your life path opens up and your purpose becomes clearer and begins to accelerate. With practice you'll become your own life guide.

CHAPTER 3

Your Life Purpose

Have you ever wondered why you're here and what the reason is for your being? Why were you born on a certain date, at a certain time, to certain parents, in a certain country, under certain planetary alignments and into an era that infused you with a specific energy? Was it all just coincidence, or has there always been a deeper cosmic plan at play?

Indeed, we all wonder why we're here and it often seems that the older we become, the more urgent our quest to discover the meaning of life. As children we have our entire, exciting life before us. Yes? Nothing seems too difficult for us to achieve if we just focus and put all of our energy into wishing something into being.

Children are so connected to soul and the spiritual dimension. They don't question their imagination or the endless possibilities of their creativity. When we can *think and act as a child does*, we're well on our way to remembering and using the talents and skills that we brought into this lifetime.

Soul is a recorder

Each individual soul has recorded upon their shimmery essence (their energy field) the imprints of memories attained and accumulated over lifetimes on Earth or elsewhere. The soul is like a great recording device where nothing goes unrecognized.

Modern-day electronics uses crystalline technology to program and retain memory, and soul works in much the same way. Your energy field (or aura) is crystalline in nature and a natural recorder. Therefore, you have unique characteristics based upon your individual experiences. These can all be tapped into and used whenever you need them. You're unique in this regard – unlike any other soul who has ever been created.

Soul has goals

Given this unique energy that you are, you have certain goals you wish to attain during each lifetime. You decide upon these goals before you incarnate into human life. These goals are based upon what you have yet to experience and what you have yet to embody of a universal and cosmic nature.

You attain these goals by using (in this human lifetime) the specific skills you've learned and remembered over lifetimes. Plus, you learn new approaches to living during your current lifetime.

Do we all have a life purpose?

Yes, everyone has a unique life purpose! Each of us will feel this purpose as an inner yearning. It shows itself as a strong desire to achieve something important with our life.

This yearning for purpose may begin at a young age – you may know exactly what you're here for and set about accomplishing it in your youth. Or you may have an inkling of what you'd love to do and what you feel you're here for, but fear creeps in and stops you from following through as an adult.

Or you may have no *conscious* idea of why you're here and no inclination to find out either. Perhaps this all changes when some life event forces you to look deeper into the meaning of your existence?

Where are you positioned along this spectrum of 'knowing'? Are you looking for your purpose, but are unsure where or how to begin? Or perhaps you already secretly know what you're here for and are just waiting for your inner resolve to rise and give you the reason to go ahead and fulfil your innate potential?

UNIVERSAL SECRET 3:
'Your natural skills are those you've practised over lifetimes.'

To help you remember why you're here, what you're good at and what your purpose is, let's go back to childhood. For it's when we're new to Earth – with a new body and a fresh outlook that's not yet weighed down by life's responsibilities – that we're closest to spirit and our purpose.

The third Universal Secret is the knowledge that your natural skills are the ones that you brought with you into this lifetime to apply and assist you in fulfilling your unique life purpose. In order to remember what your natural skills are, it's best to go back to childhood, when your connection with the cosmos and spirit was still strong.

Reconnecting with childhood

Can you remember being little? Glance back to yourself at the age of five or younger. Imagine what you looked like and how you behaved. If you can't remember, don't worry, as it does take practice. Looking at a photo of yourself as a child helps. Or you can ask someone who knew you back then for information on what you were like.

✷ PRACTICE ✷
Go back into childhood

In your mind's eye, picture yourself as a child engaging in the activities that you loved.

- What are you doing?

- What do you look like?

- Are you alone or with others?

- Are you outgoing, or more introspective?

- Do you have particular hobbies?

- What about your thought patterns?

- Are you strong-willed, outspoken, artistic, creative, cerebral, quiet, happy or sad?

- How do you interact with life and what are your ideals for the future?

Write down what you see, hear, feel and intuit.

The more often you go back into childhood in this way, the more readily your visions will come to you and the more you'll remember why you're here. The practice *A way to connect and centre before meditation* in Chapter 1 will help you connect.

For we all bring talents and skills into each lifetime. These are the abilities that seem to come to us *naturally*. Your natural skills are the ones you've honed over lifetimes, and they are the ones you'll need in order to fulfil your unique life purpose.

When I was a child I loved nothing more than to dance and sing out loud. I thought I was a really good singer, too: opera was my favourite. From the moment I could talk, I begged my mum to take me to ballet classes, as all I wanted to do was express myself through dance.

Luckily my mum nurtured my desires and allowed me to take classes in dance. We were a working-class family, but my parents made sure that both my brother and I had opportunities that they themselves had not enjoyed as children. I'm forever grateful to them for that.

So you might be wondering why, if dance was such an innate passion within me, I'm not a dancer today. Wasn't that meant to be my purpose? Well, I thought so too, until a severe knee injury at the age of 15 affected my ability to land and jump and get up on pointe for ballet. I was so sad at the time, but I knew the injury was directing me along a different path and I accepted that.

During my late 20s, while I was consciously seeking my life purpose, I went back to that time in my life when I loved to dance. I remembered what happened at my second-ever dance class when I was five years old.

After the first class I had gone home and practised the routines we had been shown, so I'd know them at week two. When I arrived at class many of the girls hadn't practised, and so they couldn't remember what we'd learned the week before. Straight away, the teacher (who I still know to this day) said to me, 'Elizabeth, take the other little girls off into the corner and show them the routine.'

I was so young and yet she immediately saw *the teacher* in me. She trusted me to show others what to do. I felt so grown up and almost as if this was what I was meant to be doing. It made me feel good to help others.

I had forgotten about this special moment of recognition at the age of five, until I started reflecting on my life and what I was good at. Remembering it showed me that it wasn't so much a dancer I was meant to become, but a teacher. Not necessarily a teacher of dance, but a teacher of life.

I remembered that I had a *natural skill* for teaching others, by nurturing and encouraging talent. As I said, this realization dawned on me because I started earnestly searching for my purpose. Once this remembrance hit me, I knew that I could teach anything; I just had to decide what it was I loved to teach the most.

Using my story as an example, can you see a little deeper into what *you* loved as a child and what you were good at? Can you look beyond the obvious to what you're actually here for? Take your time with this process; it could be that your answers won't fully come through until you've reached your lowest ebb. It could be that you need to experience a *breaking point* in order for the light to come through.

Reaching your breaking point

Spiritual seekers throughout the millennia of history have experienced the often-necessary low that must come before the dawn of insight awakens our being. Perhaps you've already been there? Perhaps you're there right now? Or perhaps this period in your life is yet to come.

One of my major breaking points came after my marriage collapsed in the mid-1990s. I was 27 – young when I look back now, yet at the time I felt I was old. I couldn't believe that the person (my husband) I had chosen to be part of my family, the one who I thought loved me and wanted to share the journey of life with me, could leave me.

It shook my personal paradigm to the core. My natural instinct was to go quiet. I withdrew my energy to think and to sink deeply into my reason for being. I still went to work each day and fulfilled my responsibilities as a project manager for a manufacturing firm. I still went to my aerobics class each night and I still taught dance teams, as I had done for more than 15 years at that stage.

Yet when I closed my door at night and on the weekends, I went still. It was an innate pull to be on my own and not be influenced by outside sources. I withdrew from my friends and most social engagements. Sometimes I'd venture out with others, but only when and if I wanted to. I can remember at the time denouncing any idea I'd ever had that there is a God or supreme intelligence in the universe. I said to myself, *I only trust in me*. I wanted to learn how to rely upon myself fully.

Have you ever reached a similar low in your life? Perhaps one that made you question everything you've ever known? Breaking points can come at any age, and often when we're least expecting them. My advice is not to be afraid of your breaking point. For indeed, it may be the catalyst you need to propel you on to your life purpose and your broader reason for being.

Waking up

In the aftermath of any major breaking point or life crisis, we have an opportunity to *wake up*. 'Wake up from what?' you might ask. Well, just consider that most people are asleep in their everyday life. By this I mean that they're not yet fully utilizing their entire consciousness to explore and expand their cosmic life path. The vast majority of us tend to be focused on our physical life, perhaps only briefly touching the soul on a daily basis.

Yet when a personal situation or a global event arises that challenges us to our core, we can find that we're forced to go within. There comes a point when we discover that our answers can't be found in the world outside us. Has this ever happened to you? Have you ever reached your breaking point?

You've probably heard of *wake-up calls*. These are moments in life when an event causes us to stop and rethink who we are, where we're heading and why we're here. It may be a health crisis, an accident, a relationship breakdown, a world event, a run-in with adversity; whatever it is for you, you'll know when your wake-up trigger arrives, for it'll cause you to stop and consider your next steps.

Waking up can take place over time

How do you know if you've woken up and if your breaking point is serious enough to cause an awakening within? Well, a sense of expansion starts to take you over when you wake up. You receive an inner knowing that personal freedom is coming. You may feel quietly excited, like I did when I first woke up.

Even though I feel the pinnacle of my wake-up call occurred on New Year's Eve 1999, my breaking point actually came on slowly, over several years before this. Yes, it was my marriage breakdown that brought my wake-up call on, but waking up was a process that developed over time, as and when I was ready.

So, waking up may not take place in an instant for you. It may develop slowly, over months or years. The waking-up process will be different for everyone. Some people will move quickly once they've reached their lowest ebb, while others will languish there. Others will pick themselves up and find themselves back at another breaking point in the future. Each time this happens we're given another opportunity to awaken to soul and our spiritual truth.

Soul doesn't judge when or how we wake up. The personality, however, may find fault in our process. That's to be expected when the head is disconnected and not aligned with the heart. The two working together as a team (soul and personality) usually occurs after we've woken up and are consciously on our *spiritual path*.

Being spiritual

So what is *your* spiritual path? It's interesting to note that most people tend to relate to being on their spiritual path *after* they've woken up. When we attend a spiritual group or a healing course, often one of the first questions we're asked is, 'How long have you been on your spiritual path?'

If this happens to you, I urge you not to feel put on the spot or unsure what to say. For in reality, we've been on our spiritual path all of our life, by virtue of the fact that we're spiritual beings. It's just that we may not have remembered who we are. Hence, after waking up, spirituality tends to take on a deeper, more personal meaning.

Let's also consider that being spiritual has nothing to do with following a religion, either. Spirituality is our *birthright*. It's the practice of being in spirit. Being spiritual is having an inner knowing that a cosmic force greater than ourselves is at work within the universe and that we're an important part of that universal energy. We're all spiritual beings and we're all spiritual at our core. It's just that some people remember and others do not.

The Acceleration

Since 2011, we've been on an accelerated path of spiritual and cosmic growth. There was much excitement about the December 2012 solstice being a herald of a new, transformative era and the end of a great astrological age. However, I felt that this great shift occurred much earlier: back in January 2011, at the time of the Egyptian revolution.

I had an innate feeling at the end of 2010 that global energy had made a major jump and literally *shifted*. I could feel an *acceleration* happening – meaning that the gap between thought and form rapidly narrowed. What previously seemed slow and laborious to manifest was now occurring at lightning speed.

Can you remember early 2011? How did that year begin for you? Did you experience an accelerated growth spurt? Did you find that your desires manifested quickly? Or perhaps many life-changing challenges came your way? Both happened for me that year, and as I look back, 2011 was one of my major turning points, both personally and professionally.

January 2011 and the ensuing 11 months saw some of the most intense natural Earth shifts for many decades. Thousands of lives were claimed by these every month in 2011: the USA experienced the largest breakout of tornadoes in its known history, and record-breaking snowstorms in the east of the country; there were landslides in Brazil, earthquakes in Christchurch, New Zealand and in eastern Turkey, a major drought in East Africa, severe floods in Bangkok, Thailand, a typhoon in the Philippines, and the Fukushima earthquake and tsunami in Japan.

Since 2011, we've been dealing with a very different energy paradigm on Earth, one that has opened up the gateway for truth to be free and people to claim their innate power. Technology has been rapidly advancing (particularly the Internet and artificial intelligence) and with this has come the opportunity to communicate with each other in an instant and share our voices like never before.

People are experiencing an increase in *ascension symptoms*, meaning that wake-up calls are on the rise and our bodies are morphing and undergoing energetic and physical upgrades. As our bodies respond to the high-vibration cosmic energy that has been infiltrating Earth since 2011, we're experiencing similar physical, emotional, mental and spiritual changes en masse.

This is such an important topic that I've devoted two sections of the book to a practical explanation of these energy upgrades – Reference Guide 1 (*see pages 67–85*) and Reference Guide 2 (*see pages 183–211*). In these you'll learn about the cosmic causes of this accelerated energy and how to work with and translate the physical symptoms that are occurring as you experience an acceleration of your life and your purpose.

CHAPTER 4

Using Your Imagination and Intuition

In Chapter 3 we touched on your unique talents and skills, as we looked at your life purpose. Is this now helping you to form an idea of what you're naturally good at? Are you naturally intuiting what soul desires for you to experience and grow from in this lifetime? Your next step is to look at making *your purpose* into a reality.

The reality of imagination

In Chapter 3 we also spoke about the brilliant capability children have to easily use and trust in their imagination and creativity. You've not lost this skill. It's innate within each of us to imagine and use our consciousness to project and paint the picture of our life.

How often do you project your thoughts into the future? Is it daily, or every so often? When you do so, what images come to you? Are you seeing a future that's positive or negative? Have you ever considered that *you* have full say over the way that your future pans out? What you experience in this moment, tomorrow and next week is down to the feelings, images and attitude that you create today.

Your imagination is real. It's a tool of spirit. We should be taught in school that using our imagination is vital for creating a life of purpose, meaning and reward. All hugely successful people use their imagination to envision the experiences they wish to bring to themselves. You're no different. So let's begin by making the decision to start engaging our imagination on a daily basis. Let's make a plan.

Your imagination exists within the spiritual dimension. It's a language of soul. You'll remember from Chapter 1 that everything in the physical dimension (the visible) comes forward first as an *idea* from the spiritual dimension (the invisible). You have to *think it* before it takes form. You're the thinker and the one who gets full say over what your physical reality becomes.

Soul and personality together

Personality and soul need to work together as a team in order for the ideas that spring forth from your imagination to take root in your everyday life. Go back and reread Chapter 2 if you need a refresh on the teamwork that takes place between heart and head.

It's soul that comes up with the original idea and gives it over to the personality to carry out. How does this happen? Well, when you allow your head to go quiet and stop overthinking, your personality immediately drops down into the heart. Soul then links up with the head and starts to emit imagery to the brain. This triggers your imagination to begin painting pictures upon the fabric of the invisible dimension. These pictures will form the framework on which your physical creations take shape.

To help your head relax so the imagination is triggered, you'll need to be still for a few moments and pause often in your day. Focus on something simple, like the Sun on your skin, beautiful music, or the warmth and taste of the cup of tea or coffee you're sipping. As you do this, you automatically switch the focus of your consciousness from the outer world to your inner world and imagination starts to rise. It's that simple.

Becoming a visionary

People with an active imagination give themselves permission to dream. *Dreamers can become doers*, and we'll look at how to make this come about in Chapter 5. Using your imagination to paint your reality is a practice that shouldn't be frowned upon, but encouraged. Someone who can imagine future possibilities is someone who is closely connected with soul. That someone can be you.

Keep in mind that from the perspective of soul and the heart, everything is happening now in a perfect field of wholeness, with no division. However, from the perspective of your personality there's a timeline of past, present and future in a universe that knows duality.

It's the task of the personality to take what's timeless – the ideas from soul – and develop it into something tangible, within a physical timeframe. This is why the head and heart are often in a quandary. One sees limitations and the other doesn't.

Soul is the originator

Does it surprise you to learn that ideas originate in the heart via soul, rather than in the brain via the personality? Have you considered that the original thinker is soul? It's delicious, isn't it? The more that we can drop our head to heart, the easier it becomes for us to imagine far-reaching possibilities for our life.

When you can naturally do this, you'll also develop a knack for coming up with original ideas. For the personality loves to copy or imitate, and soul loves to lead. Think about all of the times in your life when you tried to copy what someone else was doing. Did it work out for you or did the result seem stilted and disingenuous? What about the times when you went off on your own tangent and followed your own ideas? Did they seem more natural and progressive to you?

Visionaries are created

Becoming a visionary takes practice. A visionary is someone who uses his or her imagination in total trust. Visionaries are in direct contact with soul and see far forward and from a higher perspective as well.

Visionaries don't limit their imagination, and they know from first-hand experience that our physical reality is formed because of the pictures that we paint in our mind. Visionaries know that they're responsible for their reality, and they relish this. They've learned to harness their imagination as *the paintbox of created reality.*

Do you want to become a conscious visionary? Do you want to see a future you desire and then set about making it happen?

We're all visionaries in the making, and we all have access to an imagination that we can use to our highest advantage.

Close your eyes and say the word 'visionary'. What happens to you as you do this? How does your body respond? Does a physical feeling arise? If so, good! *Feeling* is the next vital step in taking your imaginative ideas and making them blossom.

Feeling what you can imagine

Once we've started using our imagination each day and are enjoying the process, it's important to start focusing our *desires*. Desires arise naturally from soul and the heart and they help to direct our imagination. Say the word 'desire'. Where in your body can you feel it? Is it around your heart? Desire evokes a feeling – one that carries your life purpose upon it. Desires emit amazingly condensed energy. Desires give our imagination richness, depth and scope.

I suggest that you give yourself permission to dream wildly about your life path. Why not decide to devote some time each day to imagining your future? This is where your focus will come in. You can focus on developing your imagination while conducting the daily business of your life – driving to work, sitting on a bus or in a waiting room, or while having a shower or cooking.

Soul will see to it that you can imagine at the same time as you perform daily tasks. See yourself living the life you desire, then *feel* yourself living that life. Imagine right now that you're leading your ideal life, using your natural talents and skills and fulfilling your purpose. How does it feel to be in this situation? Allow each cell in your body to tingle and vibrate to the high energy that comes in when you're doing and being what you love.

Training your personality

Now your personality may try and tell you that the life you're imagining is impossible to attain. All sorts of doubts, fears and excuses can arise. Be ready for this. It's only natural that your personality will take some convincing. After all, it's the job of your personality to look out for you in your physical life.

Your personality wants to ensure that you're not let down and that you can achieve what it is you desire. Your personality likes to be practical, as it understands that the physical dimension can have its ups and downs. So try not to be too hard on your head if self-doubt comes in. The more you can allow yourself to imagine, feel, and then act, the more on board personality becomes with soul.

If you can allow yourself to feel and act *as if* what you're imagining is happening now, the quicker your desires will shoot through the spiritual, invisible dimension and start building a physical framework of form.

Feelings enrich thoughts and supercharge our imagination. The more you can feel what it is you envision for your future, the sooner it will become physically real. This is a powerful practice for accelerating your life path.

Interpreting your imagination

So, how do you know that what you're imagining is what you're *meant* to be creating in your physical life? For sometimes we imagine scenarios that may seem far out and entirely whimsical.

For example, you could be flying through space and becoming master of a far-off star system, something that isn't feasible in your human life.

And it's OK to have amazing, fantastical dreams. They expand your consciousness and nourish the ground on which the seeds that become your reality are planted. Your personality will do a fine job of telling soul what's probable in the physical reality and what isn't.

If your imagination produces desires that are highly achievable in your human life yet may take some work, effort and time on your part, your personality will likely feel hesitant or resistant. That's a good sign. Resistance means that you're probably well on target for what your next action steps should be.

If your imagination produces desires that are *out of this world* (so to speak), your personality will look upon them as if it's watching an enjoyable movie. Your personality won't encounter resistance, for it understands that these are fun images to help you relax and expand and are not to be made into your physical reality. Can you see the difference? Chapter 8 explains momentum and resistance in great detail, for both are created in the physical universe of duality as our imagination sparks and we decide to move ahead and onto purpose.

UNIVERSAL SECRET 4:
'Your tutor within (your intuition) is the voice of soul.'

Imagination is the precursor of intuition. Intuition is also a language of soul. Once we have an idea of what it is we desire to be creating and living each day, our intuition strengthens. Intuition is generated by your *tutor within.*

Intuition is feedback on the images you're creating with your imagination. Once you start 'actioning' your imagination, your intuition gives you valuable advice about what is and isn't working for you and what needs adjusting. It's vital that you not only listen to your intuition, which can come through as an inner voice, hunches, physical instincts, dreams, conversations, signs and the like, but follow it as well.

Following your intuition

So, taking your intuition seriously is important. After all, intuition is direction from soul. It's what everyone wants – their own inner advice from the source that knows them better than anyone. Do you follow your intuition or do you second-guess yourself?

Do you even know what your intuition is? Intuition is that inner sense that something is or isn't right for you. It's a message from the spiritual dimension (the home of soul) that helps you to effectively navigate your physical life and fulfil your purpose. *Following your intuition regularly will profoundly accelerate your life purpose.*

What if you decide to trust your inner tutor (your intuition) and follow through with the ideas coming to you via your imagination? Why not take your own advice? The more you do so, the more you'll know if this advice is true for you and whether or not your intuition works in your favour. You'll learn first-hand what it is to trust in your own knowledge as you develop deep inner wisdom.

✳ PRACTICE ✳
Enhance your intuition

One of the best ways I know to improve our intuition and nourish our imagination at the same time is to *take a leap of faith*. The next time you feel your intuition talking and trying to get your attention, do the following exercise:

1. Write down what you see, feel, hear, and receive from soul, then look for instances where what you've intuited actually starts to come about.

2. If your intuition gives you a message about something you wish to share with someone close to you, then why not tell him or her? This may seem risky at first (especially to the personality) because the person you share with may not understand what you're saying.

    However, choose wisely what you say to whom and follow your gut instinct. Soul won't steer you wrong. The number of times I've felt the need to instinctively share information I've intuited and the person I shared with then gave me invaluable confirmation that my intuition was spot-on, has never ceased to amaze me. It'll work for you too. The more you do it, the more you'll come to trust.

3. It also helps if you can create an *actual physical image* of the life purpose that your imagination gives you, and

which you can see yourself fulfilling. Draw it, paint it, or create a digital image of the ideal life scenario you desire to create.

4. Place this image where *only you will see it* each day. For your inner desires are sacred and belong only to you, especially when they are in their infancy. If you can keep the energy 'tight' around what you're creating, you'll accelerate its physical manifestation. We'll speak more about this in Chapter 10, The Power of Secrecy.

CHAPTER 5

Accelerating Your Life Purpose

As we discussed in Chapter 4, nurturing your imagination is a key component and Universal Secret in uncovering your life purpose. When you trust in your imagination regularly, your intuition then works in tandem with it, picking up cues and clues along your path and advising soul and your personality on the best ways to advance.

Both your imagination and intuition need to be used and trusted (on a daily basis) for your life purpose to develop and become consciously known to you.

There's a vital next step in developing and advancing your life purpose. It also applies to anything you desire. This step is to *take action*. Once you've come up with an idea that you love and have sparked your imagination and intuition, you then need not only to *think* about your idea but also start *doing it*.

Now this is a point at which many people give up on their dreams, even before they've begun implementing them. Perhaps you've been taught or are of the opinion that it's enough just to *ask for what you desire* and that by doing this, the universe will bring it to you? So many people pray, wish and plead with the universe for help, without realizing that the next vital step is theirs to take.

Actioning your desires

'Actioning' your desires involves physically taking the steps that will see your ideas come to life. Now you don't need to have a detailed action plan before you begin – you just begin with an idea and a vision. Once you've come up with an idea and are nourishing it daily by imagining and feeling yourself living an empowered lifestyle, then your everyday life will start to get very uncomfortable if you don't *do anything* about actioning your desired lifestyle.

For soul is giving your personality these inspired ideas, which form a framework upon which your physical life starts to build. If you don't begin to use your body, your voice, your talents and skills to make *physical (and real)* what you see and feel in the invisible dimension, then the images weigh you down and you become even more frustrated and stuck than you would do if you *didn't* have a vision. Interesting, isn't it?

UNIVERSAL SECRET 5:
'You must give yourself permission to start along your path.'

This is our fifth Universal Secret. The universe waits for your call. You're the boss and you get to say when and how your life purpose pans out. Is that news to you? Does that excite you or make you nervous?

The ball is in your court. So if you sit back, thinking that what you need to experience will come to you, you may be waiting a long time. For we accelerate our life purpose by taking the reins and bringing experiences to us via our inspired actions.

How to move ahead

So, how do you know precisely which steps to take and when and how to take them in order to follow through with your ideas and dreams in fulfilling your life purpose? Which actions will you benefit from and how do you know what is yours to do and what the universe will actually take on and deliver to you?

Well, I suggest that you begin with a simple plan. Common sense works wonders when manifesting anything that you desire. It also helps if you get used to writing things down – keep a journal or a notebook in which to record your plans and experiences. The very act of writing is one of actioning ideas – taking them from the invisible dimension and making them *real* in the physical.

Form a plan

Take any idea that soul has given you about your life path. Imagine it right now. Bring a picture into your mind's eye of what you look, sound and feel like when you're living this ideal. As you do this, write down or draw what you see.

I'll give you an example. Back in 2000 I was envisioning my life purpose and what I wanted my future to be. At the time I was working full-time in a corporate environment, which I had been doing since 1991 and wasn't enjoying. I instinctively knew that I wasn't fulfilling my higher life purpose, even if I wasn't yet sure what that purpose was.

My imagination and intuition began giving me visions in which I was working for myself, in my own business, helping people all around the globe with self-development. I could envision myself getting up each day feeling excited about what was to ensue.

I'd be exercising, enjoying a leisurely breakfast and then entering my home office feeling relaxed and ready for a rewarding day – without having to drive through traffic and feel stressed by 9 a.m. That was my vision and it made every cell in my body tingle and come alive.

So from this brief I was given by soul, I decided I needed to start taking action steps if my vision was ever to come to light. One of the first things I did was to buy numerous self-development books, and I committed to reading them every week. I also started taking courses. At first, I wasn't sure which course I needed, but when a friend suggested I try one on massage, I decided it was a sign and dived in. That course led me, eventually, to discover Reiki and the world of energy healing; this was something I hadn't known about before but it was a perfect next step along my path.

I also decided that I'd need to transition out of my office work over the next few years, so I began saving more money than I was spending. I started investing in self-education that was in alignment with my visions of working in self-development. These were all positive action steps that went towards building my dreams into a concrete form. I wasn't sure exactly what each step would bring me, but I knew it would take me closer to making my visions a reality.

I took action steps based upon my visions and they gave me self-confidence and trust in myself, my talents and my born-with skills. If you'd told me back in 2000 that I'd become a professional Cosmic Guide, I probably wouldn't have known what you were talking about, but I'm sure I'd have been quietly excited.

I also remember writing down everything that I was doing and what I planned to do. Each day I'd make a new list of what I wanted to achieve – just small things like enquiring about a course I was interested in or setting up my home office. Each week, I'd cross off what I'd achieved and that made me feel so good. I'd carry forward or adjust my future plans based on what I'd actioned the previous week.

One day a friend I'd met at a spiritual centre said to me, 'Wow! You're really doing it,' as if she was surprised I was making my dreams a reality. That comment actually gave me a big boost. It also made me wonder, *How many people never follow through with their dreams? And if they did follow through, where would we be as a planet? How much happier and more at peace could we all become?*

So, can you see how important and in fact *simple* it is to start moving ahead? You don't need to know exactly what your final destination is or even how you're going to get there, you just start moving in the *general direction* of your desire. This is what grows and develops your life purpose.

Knowing the right path to take

Once you've begun taking action steps towards your life purpose, you may start to wonder if you're creating the best path for yourself, as many options can arise. Different paths can potentially show themselves to you as you start to move ahead. These are paths and options that you would never have considered if you hadn't started taking action and working towards developing your life purpose.

Keeping your life path organic

If you stay focused on the overall theme and dream that you have, you really can't go wrong when change presents itself. Rather than being rigid in your approach, I suggest that you be *organic*. Being organic along your life path means that you're open to the best suggestions that will come your way. It also means that you'll be flexible and ready for change, as and when change presents itself.

Being flexible in your action steps keeps you closely aligned with the spiritual dimension. This ensures that as new information comes to you, you're open to receiving it and aren't closed off to potential improvements that you hadn't foreseen. Soul works in fluid ways that are sometimes at odds with your physical life. Your personality may not be able to make sense of the steps that it's being pushed to take.

For example, when I first got the message to start learning massage back in 2000, my personality didn't want me to do it. My head couldn't work out what massage had to do with me working for myself in self-development. My personality was focusing on a vision in which I was teaching people with words and actions, rather than being engaged in massage.

But I went ahead and did the course anyway. Something told me I'd learn my next steps if I did. I trusted my intuition and it paid off. It was during my massage course that I met new friends who were spiritually aware. Our conversations during and after class were priceless. I also started to learn about the body, the chakras and energy. I started to form a picture of a whole new universe that I hadn't been consciously aware of before.

These were all vital experiences that prepared me (at my own pace) for a full-time spiritual lifestyle. So go with your gut feelings and take that leap of faith. One step leads to the next. In Chapters 7 and 9 I'll discuss how we work with the universal cosmic signs and how assistance comes in from our spirit guides, the Angelic Realm and the spiritual dimension.

Focusing on your life purpose

One of the best ways I know to enhance our visions and bring them to life is to walk through our day *as if* we're already living our ideal purpose.

I like to prepare for my interactions with people and my response to situations *before* they've happened. Did you know that there's no need to wait until someone is in front of you in order to hold a conversation with them? There's also no need to wait until you're in a situation for you to respond to it.

How can this be? Well, in Chapter 1, I spoke at length about energy and how the physical dimension of form and matter is first created as a thought or an idea in the spiritual dimension. Everything is energy and the past, present and future are all possibilities happening now: they're all happening *in this moment.*

Rehearse beforehand

Given this, you can choose when and how you experience what it is you wish to bring forward from spirit into form, by practising it now. For example, if I need to talk to someone about something important, I rehearse the conversation before it happens. I don't wait until I'm physically in front of them before I think about what to say.

I do this for two reasons. Firstly, if I rehearse my words beforehand, I'll be prepared, and therefore I'll feel confident, which means what I say will likely be better received and come across as more well-rounded, insightful and beneficial for us both.

Secondly, because we live in a universe of energy, imagining that you're talking to someone and they're responding is just as powerful as if it were happening in the physical reality. It's one and the same thing.

The process I'm referring to is similar to what children do when they *play-act*. Can you remember how, when you were little, you'd talk to your toys and invisible friends and imagine they were responding to you? You were living an incredible (perhaps fantastical) life that was 100 per cent real to you. I remember doing this for hours on end as a child, and I still do it as an adult to help me manifest my purpose with greater power and ease.

Make it real

Simply decide what it is you need to rehearse in order to advance your life purpose. For example, before I give a public talk, I practise it. Now that might not be anything new, but it's *the way* that I do so that makes a difference.

I set the scene in my office studio by burning incense or oils, playing soft music and making the space warm and light. This atmosphere helps me to connect with soul and what it is I want to bring through.

I make some notes about the key points I want to discuss, then I look around the room and imagine that an audience is forming. I see people's faces and I feel as if I'm on stage, ready to talk. Then I begin.

I literally go through every motion I'd make if I were giving a live talk. I speak out loud, so I can hear myself. And I imagine that the audience is responding to me and that I'm answering them. Again, I do this all out loud, as if it's happening in real time.

What this play-acting my purpose into being does is create the framework upon which physical reality hangs. By the time I'm finished, I'm buzzing and have a whole script of what I'd like to discuss. I even have my responses ready for the questions that will likely come my way. I'm feeling upbeat and excited rather than unsure about my upcoming talk. Plus, on an energetic level, I know that the people who are meant to be at that talk have already come in via the spiritual dimension and have joined with me in the rehearsal. It's a win-win situation for us all.

You'll find that the more you rehearse being prepared for situations, the more adaptable and trusting you become in your abilities in the everyday. It becomes easier to think and act on the spot, with great results.

✶ PRACTICE ✶
Be prepared

I can't overstate how simple it is to prepare for a situation by rehearsing it *as if it's actually happening*. This is vital for manifesting and accelerating your life purpose.

Let your imagination run wild and picture being in any situation that'll advance your life. You can do this at home, in the car, while out in nature or on a walk. I love the *walking and talking method* and use it daily.

- Nervous about an interview? Rehearse being there and imagine what the interviewer will say to you and how you'll respond.

- Worried about a forthcoming session with a new client? Before it happens, imagine you're walking through the whole experience.

- Concerned about a conversation with a loved one? Imagine they're actually with you and rehearse holding a two-way conversation with them.

Use this process for any situation you wish to focus on and be at peace with. The more you trust in this practice by doing it, the more you'll know that it does work and that *form follows energy*.

You'll also learn that 'calling in souls' to assist you in this practice – i.e. imagining that *you are with* the person involved in what you're rehearsing – happens via free will. If a soul chooses not to partake in this imaginary session with you, you'll get a sense of it.

If it becomes difficult to hold a conversation with another person, then pull back and just rehearse with yourself. Imagine heart is talking to head, soul to personality, and you'll achieve just as strong results.

Appreciating 'The Pause'

While fulfilling your life purpose there could be a time when the energy seems to come to a standstill and forward movement slows right down. You could be steaming ahead for weeks or months and then events seem to stop you. At first you might think that you're doing something wrong or that you need to change direction, or that life is against you for some reason. If this happens, I urge you to think again.

As you'll learn in the following chapters, we're working with cosmic energy every day and it does influence and impact upon our life purpose. There'll be days, sometimes even weeks, when you'll be integrating soul growth spurts and need to rest, as your body recovers from shifts and changes. I call these rest periods 'The Pause'. When you get paused, it's your opportunity to be still and reflect.

When you reflect, soul rises up and shows the personality how much you've matured, what you've learned and how you've grown. When we're busy putting our plans into action every day, we often forget to rest. So, during periods of energy integration, it's a gift to be on pause. Pausing and reflecting allows you to gauge how far you've come along your life path and therefore gives you a sense of satisfaction and achievement.

Why not decide to pause every so often in your day? You can do this while you're sat at your desk or in the car, while sipping a cup of tea, hanging out the washing or during whatever simple act allows you to go soft and be still. Pausing is powerful and will remind you of the soul force driving your human life ahead.

REFERENCE GUIDE 1

Common Physical Symptoms of Cosmic Energy Shifts and Accelerating Your Life Purpose

In this guide I've outlined some of the major physical changes that can occur when we're being affected and influenced by cosmic energy shifts. Our physical body can also undergo great changes when we're accelerating along our life's purpose.

I trust that you'll find this guide helpful and practical when you can find no physical cause for the way you feel. Cosmic energy can have a profound effect upon us, and I've found that some of my most popular teachings are the explanations of how our body responds to cosmic energy shifts.

To be aware when cosmic energy shifts are occurring, I suggest you follow my Tip-Off Global Energy Forecast, which can be found at https://www.elizabethperu.com

Refer to this guide regularly and come to know how your body responds to change.

Note: The information given below should not be treated as a substitute for professional medical advice; always consult a medical practitioner.

The brain and the body

The brain is a powerful tool of consciousness. Not only does it physically control your body via the nervous system, it also influences the two distinct halves of your body.

The brain's hemispheres

- The *right hemisphere* of your brain controls the *left side of your body*, from the eye down.

- The *left hemisphere* of your brain controls *the right side of your body*, from the eye down.

- The *right hemisphere* of your brain focuses on *imagination, creativity and femininity.*

- The *left hemisphere* of your brain focuses on *practicality, logic, analysing and masculinity.*

Feminine and masculine sides of the body

- The *left side* of your body (controlled by the *right brain*) is your *feminine and spiritual side.* Ailments and issues on *the left side* of your body relate to *focusing deeper into your spiritual path.*

- The *right side* of your body (controlled by the *left brain*) is your *masculine and physical side.* Ailments and issues on the *right side* of your body relate to *focusing deeper into your physical path.*

Giving and receiving sides of the body

* The *right side* of your body is your *giving and doing* side. It sends energy outward and is focused on all *physical pursuits.*

* The *left side* of your body is your *receiving and passive* side. It brings energy inwards and is focused on your *spiritual connection.*

* Your *arms and hands* represent what you *do* with your life.

* Your *legs and feet* represent the *direction* that you take in life.

Balancing both sides of the body

To balance the energy between both sides of your body, focus on the heart, which is the container of *soul essence* in the human body – *the soul chamber.*

Simply place your hands over your heart (right over left) and focus your awareness and attention into the heart centre. This simple act directs an even flow of energy around your body and centres your focus, which in turn brings forth wellness and good health.

Symptoms

Below are the ailments and issues that can occur during energy shifts and acceleration of consciousness.

Buzzing in the palm of the hand

You may notice that the centre of a palm buzzes, almost as if it's been charged up with electricity. This may last for 24 hours or more at a time and indicates that you're in an active *doing* phase of your life.

- Buzzing in the *left palm* indicates an *incoming of spiritual information* and a message that you're receiving downloads of insight. You need to use your hands to conduct spiritual energy. Consider taking up some form of energy or hands-on healing.

- Buzzing in the *right palm* indicates that you're *giving out energy* and messages to others. You're in an action phase of walking your talk and applying what you know.

Ear downloads

When we're advancing spiritually, our vibration (the rate at which our cells move) increases. We begin to accelerate and literally feel lighter and tingle all over. During any period in which your vibration increases you can also feel ungrounded and as though you're walking on air.

Vibration is movement and even when we're still we're moving, for we (like the universe) are made of sound. The more we grow and ascend in our spiritual awakening, the higher the rate at which we vibrate.

As you vibrate higher, more light is emanated from and transferred to you, and as this occurs you start hearing very high tones, much as animals do. I liken these tones and sounds to messages that we're picking up from the cosmos and the

Angelic Realm at an accelerated rate. These are messages from home, as your awareness of being a Cosmic Messenger increases (you'll learn more about this in Chapters 7 and 9).

Energetically, your ears are directly connected to your third eye and also to your heart. Indeed, the word *ear* is contained within the word *heart*. Colds and flu can affect our hearing and connection to soul (the heart) and also block our hearing and our interpretations of both the physical and spiritual dimensions.

When a general malaise affects you, you may notice that your connection with spirit is dulled. If this happens, don't be concerned. We receive many high-vibration sounds/encoded messages from spirit via our ears. These sounds come in through one ear at a time and enter as a high-pitched frequency that tunes in slowly, reaches a crescendo and then slowly tunes out. These sounds happen sporadically; they don't hurt the ear and they're not tinnitus, which is a constant ringing possibly caused by nerve damage.

When you notice a high frequency entering your ear, simply pause and be still. You're being downloaded with messages from spirit about your next direction. You won't be able to decipher the messages consciously as they come through, but in the days following a download, you'll be shown signs and indications of your next moves.

Keep your ears warm and cup your hands over them gently, sending your life force energy into the eardrum. Close your eyes and imagine that your hearing extends deep within your heart. Then do the same while you imagine that your hearing extends out to the furthest reaches of the galaxy.

These high-frequency sound messages are our connection home, to the stars and to soul. Each planetary body emits a frequency, just like Earth's resonant tone. When we tune in to these frequencies and start meditating, absorbing, growing, channelling and connecting with the universal forces, we start receiving ear downloads. They're like tune-ups from other dimensions.

When you receive an ear download, be still, close your eyes and say 'thank you'. Rest in the peace that over the coming days your life will accelerate, your psychic skills will increase, your healing abilities will deepen and the gap between thought and manifestation will dramatically shorten.

- Vibrations received through the *left ear* indicate *spiritual growth*. You're being asked to act on your intuition and trust in your divine wisdom. Your life is upgrading. The left ear is your feminine ear. These incoming vibrations bring an increase in your ability to be compassionate, wise and internally strong.

- Vibrations received through the *right ear* indicate *physical growth*. You're being asked to take on practical steps, as you go ahead and action your heartfelt plans and desires. The right ear is your masculine ear. These incoming vibrations bring you extra impetus to support your dreams.

Headaches

Experiencing headaches, particularly tension headaches in the temples, is common during periods of energy shifts and high acceleration of consciousness. If you find that tension headaches strike out of the blue, look to the current levels of solar activity, as there could be a correlation.

You may also find that you clench your teeth at night, and become a prolific dreamer. This is the body's way of trying to slow down the energy shifts taking place within you. Imagine that your body is being taken on a fast roller-coaster. Its immediate response is to tense up, to slow you down. Therefore, if you're experiencing tension or thumping headaches regularly, make sure that you increase your intake of water. This helps your cells to release tension and as a result, energy can flow through you with greater ease.

It also helps to take a salt bath using either Dead Sea salts or Epsom salts. Salt bathes you in negative ionic charge and neutralizes excess positive electrical charge in your body. Taking a salt bath is similar to walking along the beach, as a feeling of balance, release and calm ensues.

Internal heat

During periods of rapid acceleration of consciousness you may notice that you become internally hot. This is different to a physical fever. You're not actually sweating, but instead feel an internal heat – what I liken to a *spiritual fire* burning away old, restrictive patterns and toxicity from your energy field.

If this occurs, rest as much as possible. Your body is repairing and preparing you for the next phase of your life. Internal heat and energy burn-offs often happen after a period of intense searching for our direction and deeper meaning. They can also be triggered by frustration brought on by knowing what your next steps are, but being unable to take them for whatever reason.

Third-eye clearing

The pituitary and pineal glands join forces to awaken what we call our *third eye*. The pituitary is a pea-sized gland that sits behind the centre of the forehead and in between the eyes. It regulates hormone release to every major gland of the body and is a *physical gland*.

The pineal gland is a small pine-shaped gland that sits in the middle of the brain, behind the pituitary gland. It helps us to see deeply within and to access cosmic consciousness. It's a *spiritual gland*. (Have you ever looked at a pine cone and seen the eyes of wisdom contained within it?)

The third eye is a combination of these two forces and is like an inner lens into other worlds. When the third eye is activated, one can see beyond time and communicate with multidimensional beings.

The pineal gland activates and produces floods of melatonin as we tune in to the spiritual dimension. A flourishing pineal gland can induce out-of-body experiences (OBEs) and intense lucid dreaming (you'll learn all about these in Chapter 7). It helps us perceive otherworldly experiences and realms of existence. It awakens us.

The third eye, when activated, then also joins forces with the heart, the soul chamber, forming a pyramid of energy between the three centres of consciousness in our human body: the pituitary gland, the pineal gland and the heart. This is the inner trinity of wisdom and divine knowledge.

When you're accelerating in consciousness, not only does your third eye buzz and awaken, helping you to see your multidimensional reality, it also helps to actualize your inner visions, through the vessel of the heart.

If your third eye becomes hazy, disturbing your connection to the other realms, you may get a cold or blocked sinuses. If this is happens, don't worry. Allow the virus time to run its course and reset your clear focus within. Once you're over your illness, you may notice that your connection between the two glands – between the physical and spiritual dimensions – is stronger and clearer than ever. Being out in fresh air and getting lots of sleep and rest are good remedies.

Sore eyes

When you're advancing in conscious awareness, it's common to experience sore, weeping or even dry eyes. The cosmic climate will be pushing you to look deeply into issues that you've perhaps avoided seeing for far too long. You may notice that one eye or the other is bloodshot, swollen, gritty or weepy.

- Your *left eye* is your *spiritual eye*. It sees into your past and past lives and the soul. Look into someone's left eye if you want to make a heart connection. What are you consistently thinking about? Is it the past? Are you listening to your heart?

- Your *right eye* is your *physical eye*. It sees into future possibilities and the personality. Look into someone's right eye if you want to make a direct (here and now) connection. Are you afraid of seeing into your future? Are you taking direct action?

Sore feet

During energy shifts our physical and spiritual direction are of top priority. You may notice that your feet become sore, stiff or tight. This can often happen when we're unsure of our next steps, even though we know we're in the process of moving ahead.

Likewise, if you're feeling stuck and unsure in your life, your heels in particular can become very sore or even grow plantar warts. Such skin conditions on the bottom of the feet can indicate a *deep displeasure* at the next steps you're taking.

You may also be going through an incubation stage with your direction, and feel the need to stand still for a while as you assess what your next steps will be. Bunions on the feet can indicate displeasure at where you're heading, or the need to be more grounded in your approach.

Fungal infections around the toes, such as athlete's foot, can represent an itching desire to forge your own path. And yet you may feel as though someone or something is holding you back.

The toes support the entire weight of the human body and help us to balance. If you break or injure your foot or toes, ask yourself if you're feeling unsupported by the world around you. You would do well to realize that *you are* always going to be your greatest ally, supporter and guide.

Our feet take such a hammering every day. They carry our entire physical and energetic weight, and therefore it's so important to treat them with the care and dignity they deserve. Hold your feet in your hands and tell them that you *love them*. Tell your feet how proud you are of them for doing such a wonderful job in walking you through your life, even when you're unsure of where you're going or why.

Salt baths are wonderful for draining negative or toxic energy out of your feet at the end of the day. Massaging your feet with body cream or oil (not between the toes) is also a sacred way to nourish and give thanks to this most vital part of your body for your forward direction.

Sore knees

The knees are the bridge between the spiritual and physical dimensions. They're like way showers on our path. The knees take on the indication of our direction in life and how well we forge ahead or resist progress out of fear. The knees pass information between what we desire and how we can make that desire *manifest*.

When we doubt ourselves as we accelerate, particularly about where we're heading, our knees can possibly take a hit. They'll swell or the cartilage can crunch and wear away. In severe cases of self-doubt along our path, the knees may dislocate, forcing us to stop and no longer move ahead.

- *Left knee issues* can indicate doubt over your *spiritual path*. The ancient Egyptians would always walk with the left foot forward, showing their connection with spirit. Look at any ancient Egyptian statue or relief and you'll see the left foot pointed ahead of the right, walking with spirit leading.

- Left knee issues can also relate to using your creativity and intuition to get ahead. Perhaps you're holding back your skills?

- *Right knee issues* can indicate doubt over your *physical path*. You may not like taking action and doing what needs to be done in order to get you where you desire to go. You may despise harder physical work. Perhaps you push and over-control your direction?

If your knees are of concern, I suggest that you start believing in yourself more. You can do this by following through with your deepest desires for your life. Rather than just thinking about what life would be like if you were living up to your visions, take the first steps in making them happen. Belief grows from hands-on, personal experience. Prove your worth by having the courage to stand up for yourself and your desires.

Shaking, weak or knocking knees can be eliminated when you feel the energy planted firmly into your feet, rather than being blocked at the kneecaps. Focus on each step you take quite literally, rather than just seeing the bigger picture. Break down your desires into bite-sized steps and make them happen.

Sinus problems

During periods of accelerated energy your nose may be affected – it may become red, sore, blocked or runny. This can be because your third-eye connection is clearing (*see third-eye clearing, page 74*).

Excessive sneezing (aside from seasonal allergies) can also indicate that you're letting yourself down on some level. When we sneeze we can be covering up for our feelings of inadequacy. After a big sneeze, pause for a moment and consider what you were thinking about just beforehand. Can you see a correlation between the sneeze and a thought in which you doubted or undervalued yourself?

Try breathing through one nostril at a time:

1. Place your right index finger over your right nostril, blocking the airflow. Then breathe deeply in and out through your left nostril, eight times. This will clear your right brain and left ear.

2. Next, place your left index finger over your left nostril, blocking the airflow. Then breathe deeply in and out through your right nostril, eight times. This will clear your left brain and right ear.

Sleeplessness

As we accelerate in consciousness we can expect to be *more awake than asleep*. Quite literally this translates to sleeping for fewer hours each night and/or experiencing broken sleep patterns. Get used to this new way of being, for I've found that the more aware we become, the less sleep we actually need.

Soul is vying for your attention while your body is resting, so do your best to be physically active during the day. This will ensure that your body is spent at day's end and that you're in the best position to receive some deep sleep time.

As well as restless or light sleep, you may notice that you're waking up at the same time each night – perhaps a double-digit time, like 2:22, 3:33 or 4:44 a.m. When you start seeing double-digit number sequences often, it's no accident. Once they start, they will come in succession and quickly (I cover number sequences in detail in Chapter 9, Noticing The Signs).

Spiritual flu

Acceleration of cosmic energy produces big energy shifts here on Earth, which can bring on a conglomeration of physical issues all at once. Major energy shifts on a planetary level change the vibration of our energy body (our aura), which in turn causes our physical body to experience a shedding or detox process. I call this process *spiritual flu*.

The physical body is often the last level of our being to upgrade after our energy body does. As it does so, it can produce flu-like symptoms. Major cosmic energy shifts cause an *ascension process* to take place. This means that we wake up to a higher awareness of who we are and our place within the universe as Cosmic Messengers.

Symptoms of spiritual flu can include tight muscles, tension headaches, tiredness, sore eyes, blocked ears or nose, feeling hot from within (but not experiencing fever), heat and buzzing coming from the hands and feet, tingling all over, a sore throat, loss of voice and thymus palpitations. There are many symptoms that arise seemingly out of the blue. In other words, you can't pinpoint a physical event or reason that brought them on.

During a bout of spiritual flu, you may think you're coming down with a cold or regular flu, yet you don't get the full-blown sore throat or fully inflamed sinuses and aching joints, and so on. You have some physical symptoms yet they're milder in nature than with a physical flu. Naturally if you're physically ill, do get this checked out. Always check out the physical so you can put your mind at rest.

During bouts of spiritual flu, which can often happen when you're waking up or going through a major energy upgrade proccss, listen to your body and make changes as you need to. Drink more water, stretch and rest. You're undergoing a transformation.

Stiff neck/shoulders

I often say that our shoulders represent our *shoulds* in life: we shrug our shoulders and say, 'I should do this' or 'I should do that'. Yet our shoulds are often our unfulfilled desires.

When we fail to meet our desires, and what we need for growth and personal satisfaction, we can become stooped and round-shouldered. It's as though, like Atlas, we carry the weight of the world upon our shoulders. The same can be said of sore shoulders: the muscles there can store resentment and hence cause lingering pain.

We tend to get a stiff neck when we're way too inflexible with the energy shifts that cause our life to accelerate. If you like to control your path and resist any change brought on via the universe's help, then you may often have a sore or tight neck.

I find the best way to free up your shoulders and neck is literally to notice where you're looking and where your consciousness is focused. Is it often down at the ground? Or perhaps your gaze is focused for most of the day on your computer or other technological device?

Instead, do your best to look up or at eye level as often as possible. As you do this, expand your chest so that it's open, and feel your shoulders naturally roll back – they may resist at first, because they're tight. The more you do this, the more positively minded you'll become, as you drop the shoulds and replace them with the *I ams* – for example, 'I am capable', 'I am worthy', or 'I am flexible'.

Crying

As cosmic energy accelerates, one way in which the body naturally releases tension and old energy is via the process of *crying*. When the water is flowing in our body it's easier for us to cry naturally.

Often, we can hold back our true feelings and emotions and resist tearing up. Yet the body needs a good cry regularly, not only to keep our eyes clear and bright, but also to release excessive tension in the body's cells.

Crying is a *whole body experience*. When you experience a deep cry you can feel every energy centre of your body release and heal. It's almost akin to having a therapeutic massage. You feel quite empty afterwards and perhaps still inside. Crying gives us a total body reset.

Now if you cry spontaneously, all of the time, this is different to the tears brought on by an accelerated energy shift. Constant crying could indicate that you're having trouble assimilating the changes that are happening to you. I suggest that you closely monitor your physical responses to life shifts. Make changes as they arise, and take action rather than pushing aside your true feelings, as you let it all out in a constant flood of tears.

Thymus fluttering

I often speak about the thymus – a butterfly-shaped gland that sits in the centre of our chest – and how it activates and literally *turns on* during periods of accelerated cosmic activity.

The thymus sits over an energy centre known as our *high heart*. The high heart is akin to a gateway from the heart chakra to the throat chakra. It vibrates to the colour turquoise, which is a mixture of green and blue.

As we open up to soul and greater love, this energy centre awakens. As energy passes up, on its way to be expressed via our voice, the thymus will quite literally *flutter*. You may sometimes feel this centre activate when you're finding your true voice and speaking from a place of soul and love. During periods of heightened Earth and spiritual awakening, it's common for our thymus to grow.

The ancients taught us that the thymus is our gland of *spiritual awakening*. When we grow spiritually and connect to our source, the thymus flutters like a butterfly and is actively vibrating as it transforms us into knowing spiritual beings. As we get older, rather than going into atrophy, the thymus awakens and thrives, especially the more spiritually aware we become.

When your thymus flutters it can be mistaken for heart palpitations. Of course, if you're having flutters in your chest, get this checked out by your doctor to put your mind at rest; however, I've heard from many people who have had their hearts checked, only to be told there were no issues. They were relieved to discover that the source of their chest fluttering could have been the thymus awakening.

When the thymus gland is fluttering you can tap over it to calm it; this also works to awaken it when you're feeling flat. Using your index and middle fingers together, make some gentle taps over the small indent in the centre of your chest, just under your collarbone. This soothes the rhythm of the thymus and can relax the fluttering process.

Tight muscles, torn ligaments and broken bones

Our muscles store memory – in particular they can be brilliant at storing unexpressed emotions. The emotions we tend to hold in are usually the negative ones that we're too scared to express. Pulled, tight or ripped muscles can be the result of a build-up of negative emotion.

Notice which part of your body is sore or tight during accelerated energy shifts. Reflect upon what repetitive thinking or old habits arising from your resistance to letting go could be causing the pain.

Ligaments join bones together and provide stability within the body and between the body parts they're connecting. If your ligaments are stretched or torn, look at which parts of your body they are joining. Are you overworking this area of your body or putting too much strain on it?

Bones are the basis of our innate structure and form. An issue with your bones can represent energy that goes back a long time, even lifetimes. Like muscles, bones store emotions, very deep-seated ones. By the time an emotion moves into your bones it's been sitting in your muscles for a long time.

Breaks or fractures of bones can represent a sudden cutting off of the old emotion. In short, breaks or fractures can free the old emotion and allow you to *reset* yourself. To avoid a break or fracture, do your best to address the old emotions you're keeping locked up inside before they advance.

As muscles, ligaments and bones store memory, it's important that any negative emotional experiences be addressed *as they happen*, rather than left to sit in your body. I suggest that you become very aware of what your body is saying to you, as the little aches and pains arise. Address them while they're small, so they don't become too large to handle.

Talk to your body each day. Ask it how it feels and how you can help to make your thinking more in alignment with your body's desires. Also, after any injury or illness, focus your mind into that body part and ask, *Why did that happen?* Your body's intelligence will direct you as to the cause and speak to you in clear terms. You'll love the wisdom that you receive from this practice of *body talk*.

PART II

*Becoming a
Cosmic Messenger*

CHAPTER 6

Planetary Bodies and You

Let's now delve in even deeper and venture far out too, as we expand our awareness to *the cosmic level*. Have you ever looked up to the stars at night and wondered about your place in the universe? I have, for my whole life, and it was while doing this on New Year's Eve 1999 that I had my most profound *conscious wake-up experience*.

There's something about looking up at the stars that connects us to a higher purpose, and to latent soul memories of being at home among the cosmos ourselves. After all, is there anything truly as fascinating as what lies beyond our human comprehension?

What is a planetary body?

Consider that each planet in our solar system is a body – one just like yours. In Chapter 1 we explored the human body and you learned that we're made of energy and are created as souls that are free to incarnate in any form we choose.

Right now you're experiencing a human life and your soul is creating your physical body. Imagine that planetary bodies are the same. There's a soul creating them too, just like you. Each planet can be considered a body with a soul; it's on a larger scale than yours, but it's a body and soul nonetheless.

UNIVERSAL SECRET 6:

'Each of us is a planetary body.'

This means that each planet has a divine consciousness creating, forming and shaping it, just like you do. Given this, our next Universal Secret is that each of us is a planetary body. In fact, every living being that has a physical form could be considered a planetary body. Does this give you greater respect for every life form, knowing that we each carry great weight and responsibility within the cosmic dance of life?

Planetary bodies impact on each other

Just as we're all planetary bodies, we all impact on each other. Your body's presence and energy field (aura) interact with those around you. Depending on the strength of your energy field, you could literally influence thousands of other beings on a daily basis.

Now consider the energy field of a planet. Jupiter is almost 1,300 times larger than Earth, and although it's millions of kilometres from Earth, its energy field is immense and radiates out into our solar system, affecting and interacting with other planetary bodies as it does so. We're quite literally impacted by Jupiter's presence and the more we attune with this cosmic influence, the more we interact with it and evolve because of it.

Just as we can use our imagination to practise being on purpose, so too we can imagine what it's like to experience life on other planets. We can literally beam our consciousness to any planet we desire (via the spiritual dimension) and by focusing our energy field, feel and interact with the presence of another planetary body.

The planets are constantly communicating with us, just as we are with them. As you become more aware of energy and use your ability to extend your presence in and out of your body, the easier it becomes to pick up the messages of the cosmos and become a Cosmic Messenger yourself.

How does cosmic energy influence us?

So, how exactly are we influenced by cosmic energy, and how different is it to our own energy? Well, cosmic energy encompasses the entire universe and is multidimensional in nature. Therefore, everything is affected by the cosmos, which we can consider to be our home.

Earth is not immune to cosmic energy. Earth is a part of the cosmos and is also cosmic in nature. Have you ever considered that you live in a cosmic universe? As we're about to discuss in Chapter 7, not only are you an inhabitant of a cosmic universe, you're also a *cosmic citizen*.

There are no physical boundaries around Earth; however, there are energetic ones. Yes, we do have an outer atmosphere that filters cosmic radiation to a certain extent. However, much cosmic energy permeates Earth's field and when it does, it interacts with our body electrics and can sink into Earth's core.

This is why we often see an increase in seismic activity when solar flaring produces geomagnetic storms on Earth. These storms give rise to auroras, and in my experience, when Earth is being bombarded by cosmic radiation, empaths and people sensitive to energy experience actual physical symptoms. Reference Guide 2 (*see pages 183–213*) explains the physical shifts that can happen to us because of planetary movements and influences.

The patterns of cosmic energy

As each physical planet moves around its centre, or its soul, the lines of energy that extend outwards form unique patterns and alignments with other planetary bodies. This is where the study of astrology comes in, for long ago in antiquity, stargazers recognized that planetary energy impacts us here on Earth.

By observing the alignment of planets and stars, patterns begin to form. Invisible lines of energy form intricate geometries. These patterns bring with them certain attributes, which repeat when and as the pattern forms and re-forms.

For example, when a planet is in retrograde motion (when it appears to move backwards around the Sun from our perspective here on Earth), we can observe and experience that life tends to slow down. We repeat the past and get the opportunity to go over old lessons. We take a backwards glance over our life because of the energy pattern formed by the planetary movement.

Physical planetary bodies have an impact on your physical body by virtue of the fact that you inhabit a physical dimension. Just imagine the impact that the Sun has on your life. This huge star, which emanates solar radiation and gives rise to life on Earth, is well over a million times larger than our planet. It's immense and its energetic effect is felt here.

The cosmic weather

We're all affected by the weather, and likewise, we're all affected by cosmic energy. It's one of my dreams that one day, every nightly TV news broadcast will not only feature an Earth weather report but a cosmic one too. I'd love to deliver that to the people of Earth. How useful would that be?!

The impact of cosmic energy on our human life is an important influence on the decisions we make and the life path we carve out for ourselves. It's why I began writing The Tip-Off Global Energy Forecast back in 2003 (*for more on this, see the book's Introduction*). Early in my holistic career I could feel that the planets had a huge impact on our physical body, and if we knew what to expect with the daily alignments, we could use these cosmic influences to our advantage.

Forming a relationship with the planets and stars

So, given that the planets have energetic fields that interact with our own, it's possible to form a personal relationship with the planets and the stars. Each of us is a unique being, with different experiences and a different energy field that we each emit. We all vibrate differently, creating a *unique song or soul signature* as we do so.

The higher we vibrate, the physically lighter we become. Each planetary body vibrates at a different rate, so there'll be some planets and stars that we attune with and others that we don't. Of course, this can change, because our vibratory rate is always shifting, as is that of the cosmos and all other planetary bodies.

So there'll be some planets and stars that you resonate with and others that you find challenging – just as you prefer some people over others. It's all in the energy. I'm not an astrologer and I've never studied formal astrology, although I did follow basic astrological premises for years. It wasn't until I started writing The Tip-Off Forecast that I began to form a very different, *intuitive* relationship to the planets and stars than the traditional teachings offered.

I began to use my intuition when connecting with planetary energy. I decided literally to *talk to the planets* I was writing about each week. I'd imagine I was holding a direct conversation with them and then ask how different cosmic events would affect us here on Earth.

At first I was quite shocked by what I heard, as I was receiving what felt like original information about planetary movements. I began to share what I brought through and it started to resonate with people. The more that I shared in my weekly forecasts, the more on point the information seemed to be. This led me to trust in the relationships that we can build up with each planetary body. I encourage you to do the same by adopting the following practice:

✶ PRACTICE ✶
Talk to the planets

Imagine that you can talk to your planet of choice and hold a conversation with it.

- You might like to ask it, 'How do you influence my life?' Or, 'What messages do you have for humanity?'

- Write down what you hear and test out the accuracy of the messages you receive for yourself.

- First-hand experience is the greatest teacher. The more you extend your energy to meet that of another planetary body, the easier it becomes to do so and the clearer your messages will be.

CHAPTER 7

Cosmic Awareness

As we touched on in Chapter 6, Earth is a cosmic planetary body. You live upon a cosmic world and are part of the cosmos yourself. It's often easy to forget this in our everyday life – we can become so focused on the physical and material aspects of living, such as going to work each day, dealing with survival, interacting with family and friends and feeling as if we're on a treadmill.

It's only every so often that we have our bubble burst by a challenging event that makes us look up and ponder the bigger picture of life and the universe. When those moments of awareness happen and you have an awakening or an epiphany (no matter how brief), it's important to pause and feel the energy, so that you *remember the moment*. These moments of awareness are recorded upon soul, and the more that we have them, the easier it becomes to attune to the cosmos and our place within it.

Just imagine that this dense Earth that you stand upon is part of our cosmic solar system. You're living upon a cosmic planet, a sphere in space. There's no roof above us and we're revolving around our Sun in a cosmic dance with other planetary bodies. We're not a planet or species unto ourselves; we're part of the whole cosmos. *Earth is cosmic.*

If you were to arrive on Earth from another planet you would be in awe of the rich diversity of life found here. Do this now. Close your eyes and imagine that you're coming to Earth for the very first time. How are you arriving? What are you sensing? Are you just observing or are you mingling with those you meet on Earth? What does this planet tell you and what can you learn from it?

The more often we remind ourselves of how important Earth is, and how we are a part of the greater whole, the more respect and honour we'll show for this cosmic body that nourishes our body and soul. Tell yourself each day that *Earth is cosmic* and see what a difference this makes. Indeed, wonder and joy will fill you up as you do so.

You are a cosmic citizen

As we come into a higher awareness that Earth is cosmic, let's also consider that we're *cosmic too.* We're often taught that Earth and humanity are distinct from the cosmos, but actually quite the opposite is true.

It's an Earth-centric view to think that we're the centre of the universe and that everything out there and beyond us is cosmic, as if somehow we're not. The more that you awaken to the multidimensional universe, the more you'll understand that we're each a part of the cosmos and that we're all *cosmic citizens.*

A cosmic citizen is someone who is aware that other dimensions exist and who takes responsibility for their energy and the influence they have upon the universal tone. As we awaken to who we are – that is, souls experiencing life through the vehicle of humanity – we naturally start to expand our experiences to take in the full range of environments around us.

Your growing cosmic awareness

You may notice that as your cosmic awareness grows you become interested in space, the planets and the stars. You may start following energy forecasts or astrology reports and as you do so, you expand your awareness of the spiritual dimension. It's when we also look for the deeper connection between all living beings that we start to recognize that we're not alone in the universe and that we're all part of one cohesive whole.

As cosmic citizens we're not confined to the Earth plane. We're eternal travellers, spiritual beings who can project our energy wherever we wish. Close your eyes and ask yourself, *What is a cosmic citizen and how do I become one?* Allow the words or feelings you receive to come through naturally and then write down what you intuit.

What does soul tell you about your cosmic reality? Does being *cosmically minded* enable you to stretch past any self-imposed limits? Is being a cosmic citizen an infinite experience?

The more you embrace your cosmic origins, the more grounded you become on Earth. Why? Well, because you're not trying to escape or run away from Earth and go off to some faraway, perhaps more enlightened, world. You realize that you already have access to any dimension and sphere of reality that you can practise attuning to – right here, while you're on Earth.

Cosmic citizens have a greater sense of camaraderie with all beings and a great empathy, sensitivity and compassion for all life forms. Cosmic citizens also become aware that they are *messengers for the universe*. You'll notice that your telepathic and psychic skills naturally increase, the more your consciousness expands, and that you encompass wholeness.

UNIVERSAL SECRET 7:
'Think and act cosmically.'

As cosmic citizens we become aware that every thought and action we carry out has influence, not just on Earth but also beyond. Someone who considers their impact before they act makes more empowered decisions and accelerates their life purpose.

Our seventh Universal Secret is to think and act cosmically. When we can do this, we automatically open up to the invisible dimension and all of the assistance available to help us grow and thrive via our human life.

When I asked soul for a title for this book, I did so by lying down on my healing table in my meditation room at home. I put on some beautiful music, lit a candle and closed my eyes. I didn't focus on any one thing, other than allowing my consciousness to expand into the cosmos and go where it needed to be.

After about 30 minutes I opened my eyes and the word *cosmic* came to me, followed by the word *messengers. What a perfect title for my book*, I thought. I thanked soul and then became quietly excited. For indeed, I realized that each day I was being a Cosmic Messenger with my writing and teaching of energy forecasts. It's a term I hadn't used before, but soul was right (as always), as it fits in perfectly with what I was about to write and share with you, Dear Reader.

We are all messengers

Each of us is already a messenger. Every day we share our thoughts, our dreams, our aspirations, our fears, our highs and our lows, whether silently within or with those around us. And with the advent of social media, we're sharing like never before.

Now how often do you stop and consider using discernment before you share? Are you a messenger of inspiration? Are you a messenger of encouragement? Or are you a messenger of doom and gloom? Do you think about what you're sharing and the impact it has, or do you just let it all out? What if you saw yourself as a Cosmic Messenger? How differently would you share?

The more aware you become of your ultimate place as a soul traveller within the universe, the better developed and holistic your outlook becomes. This takes practice of course, and as you follow the words, suggestions and techniques in this book, you'll automatically be communicating with soul and your higher guidance. This will accelerate your progress and enrich the messages that the cosmos has to share with you.

✴ PRACTICE ✴
Daily connection with the cosmos

Start putting aside some time each day to consciously commune with the cosmos. You might do this first thing in the morning or before you go to sleep at night, while out on a walk or relaxing in a warm bath, or perhaps as you just sit or lie still.

1. Close your eyes and imagine that your energy is extending beyond your body and meeting the cosmic flow. Just be in the experience and allow images and feelings to come and go as they will.

2. When you feel ready, open your eyes, place your hands in prayer position over your heart and say 'thank you'. This hand position balances your above and below energy flow and shows gratitude to the multidimensional universe of which you're a part.

3. Then, as you go about your day, notice if you start speaking differently. Perhaps your voice will deepen; perhaps you'll say less, as you listen more? You may start to feel guided in what you say, and you may also start to feel centred, as your wisdom grows.

Being a Cosmic Messenger is something that develops over time. Some people call this channelling, yet it's not necessarily another being's message that you'll speak and pass on, but quite literally the message of your own immense cosmic soul.

Your spirit guide

In Chapter 1 I spoke about the invisible and visible dimensions and the realm of spirit and the physical, both of which we inhabit. As souls embodying human lives we have a foot in two worlds. We're born of the spiritual dimension (the invisible to the physical) and we choose to travel into and manifest through the physical dimension (the visible to our human senses).

As souls and energy beings our home base is cosmic and spiritual. Do you have memories of your experiences in the spiritual dimension, when you weren't incarnate in a physical body? Perhaps you have flashbacks of what life is like without a physical body? Indeed, many of us experience this first-hand while we're sleeping and having astral travel and/or out-of-body experiences. I'll address this phenomenon later in this chapter.

The dimension of spirit is similar to the dimension of physicality, although the base vibration is higher and souls have their cosmic awareness intact. Therefore, honour of one another and the universal flow is natural in the spiritual dimension. The spiritual dimension exists in wholeness and is undivided, unlike the physical dimension.

While in your human body, soul exists in spirit. You never fully leave the spiritual dimension and can access it through meditation, sleep and by raising your daily cosmic awareness. Consider the spiritual dimension as home and a place where your soul family and greatest supporters exist.

For you're never alone on your journey through life. It may seem that way at times, especially when you face great challenges, yet there's always *a guide with you*. Soul guides your personality throughout your human life and there are guides assigned to soul to give you an ever-broader perspective on your life purpose.

Our teachers and friends

Just as we go to school on Earth to learn and prepare for our adult life, so too do we enter school within the spiritual dimension. Schooling helps us hone our natural skills and teaches us discipline and mastery of universal laws. Of course we can't learn everything in school, and that's why we can choose also to learn by creating human lifetimes for ourselves.

Those souls who have mastered repeated lifetimes on Earth and elsewhere graduate to become teacher souls. This is one of the highest levels a soul can attain and is something that each of us aspires to, even if we're not aware of it in our daily life. *The teacher and the tutor within you are strong.*

Each of us has a spiritual teacher assigned to us throughout our human lifetime. These teachers are what we often refer to as our *spirit guide*. Spirit guides are not incarnate in human form, but remain fully in the spiritual realm and assist us with higher-level (cosmic) guidance along our entire lifespan.

We can have more than one spirit guide and sometimes specialist guides come and go from our life, depending on our changing needs and spiritual growth. However, I've found that we have *one special spirit guide* who remains with us throughout our lifetime. You may have spoken and interacted with this guide as a child and not realized it. Perhaps they were your special imaginary friend?

I had an imaginary friend as a child: her name was Mary and we would speak for hours and hours. She was 100 per cent real to me and I can recall being completely oblivious to people hearing me talking out loud with my best friend Mary. Can you remember if you had a similar friend who comforted you when you were little?

Spirit guides are just like us in that they have lived human lifetimes and are very aware of the challenges of the Earth environment. It's likely that your spirit guide has lived human or other lifetimes right alongside you at some point. In your current lifetime they're in spirit and you're in the physical. Before you decided to incarnate into this lifetime, you would both have agreed to work with one another to advance your experiences of the cosmos.

Connecting with your spirit guide

To consciously connect with your spirit guide it helps to be open to that which you can't intellectually explain. It helps to have an enquiring soul and to enjoy surprises, as well as receiving assistance with your daily life issues.

If you try and do everything yourself, your guide may never get the chance to be made known to you. It's when we throw our hands up and ask the universe for help that we open the portal to the spiritual dimension and our guides can step in. For spirit guides respect one another and you, and won't provide help (or give suggestions) until you ask them to. Therefore, consciously connecting with your spirit guides is up to you. It's your call.

In order to connect with our guide we need to be open to being helped. Are you open? Are you ready to work hand in hand with the spiritual dimension? To accelerate your life purpose it dramatically helps to work with your spirit guide. Together, you become a powerful team.

Teamwork increases your cosmic powers. You can affirm this right now by saying out loud: 'Yes! I wish to work with my spirit guide as a team.' You may then get a sense that your spirit guide is coming in close to you. You may feel a tingling along your arms or back as this occurs, or you could see an image or sparkles out of the corners of your eyes.

Your spirit guide is just like you: remember this. Talk to them as you would a best friend. You may at first feel as if you're talking to yourself. Yet the more that you ask your guide for assistance, the easier it becomes to distinguish their messages as being distinct from your own intuition and soul's inner guidance.

You must do the work

You can ask absolutely anything of your spirit guide. No request is too small or too huge. That's what they're here for. But do keep one thing in mind: it's you who has to undertake any suggested work or solutions to pressing issues.

Your guide can only advise and suggest. It's up to you to action what you choose. If you choose not to action any guidance you receive, that's OK. Your guide doesn't judge; they know it's not easy living on Earth because they've been here too.

I suggest that you start by asking *simple questions* each day. You might want to know your guide's name and what they would look like if they were in physical form. This gives you a tangible frame of reference through which to connect with them.

You can ask for guidance on what food is good for you; for clarification on your own intuition; for help in speaking more clearly; for creating healthy relationships; or for remembering and using your talents and skills. Whatever your question, ask away and decide what you'll do with the advice you receive. I always thank my guide after any conversation, as this creates a strong energy field for materializing that which we've discussed.

Loving advice

Spirit guides will only ever give loving and empowering advice. By this, I mean that they won't be negative or derogatory. If you receive this type of advice it's highly likely that it's not your guide you're connecting with, but a lower (often mischievous) thought form. They do exist and can be attracted to any fear that you carry.

If you receive this type of negative message, then ask your guide to step in and clear the space. You'll feel an instant positive shift as you do this. It's also important to trust in yourself throughout the process of discovering and working with your spirit guide. Trust that you'll make a strong connection.

Spirit guides can seem to have a personality (just as you do) because they are soul, just like you. So you may encounter spirits with a great sense of humour. This is always a good sign that you've pierced directly through to the spiritual dimension.

When connecting with your guide, steer clear of negative people and unhealthy environments. If you get an uneasy feeling around someone, trust in it and move yourself clear. You can also ask to be surrounded in love and light when connecting with your guide.

Cleanse and clear your energy field (aura) with essential oils during any conversation with your guide, until you get into the flow of connecting. Just take a few drops of your favourite essential oil, rub it between your fingers and then waft it with your hands through your aura. Mostly, make your connection a joyful one. Expect advice that will help you to elevate to the level your soul came here to achieve.

And if you so choose, keep your spirit guide's advice private. As I will address in Chapter 10, *the power of secrecy* is one of the most important Universal Secrets for accelerating your life purpose.

The Angelic Realm

Also existing within the spiritual dimension, although somewhat higher in authority than the spirit guides, are the beings of the *Angelic Realm*. You might not think of there being levels in spirit, but I've come to know that a hierarchy does exist in the spiritual dimension, just as it does here in the physical.

We can think of the Angelics as pure light beings that have never incarnated into human form. They are the overseers of the spiritual dimension and are responsible for harmony within the entire universe. Angelic beings are of the highest order and they can work with your spirit guide to hone and focus your life purpose.

In my experience, the Angelics are beings of incredible power and immense wisdom. They're not pushovers. They always see the bigger cosmic picture and help hold us to account. Unlike the earthly images that often portray Angels as soft beings with fluffy white wings, the Angelics I've met and interacted with are unlike this: they're on a mission and they know exactly what their role is.

Their presence is huge and yes, I do sense a wing-like energy emanating from them. There's no doubting them and no question about who they are and what they're capable of. When they come in to assist you, your life will accelerate as never before.

Aspects of the Angelic Realm

There's order within the Angelic Realm, just as there's divine order within the universe. I sense definite levels of experience within this realm. Just as we souls are growing, learning and elevating ourselves up the spiritual ladder of evolution, so are the Angelics.

You've probably heard of the different orders of Angels. While I don't focus on these too much, I'm aware of the overriding Archangels, whose presence commands each Angelic team or arm. The Archangels are in charge of legions of Angelic beings. The Archangels are top-level assistance and in my experience are contacted when our personal Angelic guide needs to call in the big guns, so to speak.

As I said, there are different arms of the Angelic forces, and each one is responsible for a different aspect of universal order. Therefore, countless Angelic beings work under the guidance of each Archangel.

Depending on your energy and your experiences in life, you'll attract a specific Archangel team to assist you. For example, you may be highly creative and intuitive and therefore attract the Angelics who specialize in this area. Or you may favour logic and precision and therefore attract the Angelics who are aligned with this energy.

Your Angelic guide

So, how do you know if the Angelic Realm is guiding your life? We've spoken about spirit guides and yes, spirit guides are different to Angelic guides. The way I can tell the difference is this: spirit guides tend to be more dominant in our life *before* we've woken up to our cosmic nature.

So, even though you might not be aware of their presence for most of your life, your spirit guide is still with you, silently helping to adjust your course, especially if you're about to be challenged.

Once you wake up and start remembering about your soul and your life purpose, your Angelic guide becomes more vivid in your life. This is when we start to consciously connect and ask for higher-level guidance along our path.

Once you've woken up to your spiritual nature, there will come a time when your spirit guide needs to call in your Angelic guide to help take you to the next level of your soul's growth. The Angelics have access to the wider universal picture and plan unfolding – which even your spirit guide doesn't have – and hence their assistance is invaluable along your life path.

I find that the Angelics especially come in to assist those who have chosen a role on Earth of some influence. Whether that influence is teaching, leading, being in the public eye, quietly conducting energy work or setting an example by overcoming obstacles in their life, those who can influence others are always overseen by the Angelics.

You may feel the Angelic Realm coming in, as a pull to use your life as an example. You may be driven to follow a calling that involves putting others' needs ahead of your own. Many who work closely with the Angelic Realm experience a sense of self-sacrifice in some area of their life. Has this ever happened to you?

The self-sacrifice I refer to involves taking the higher ground, rather than lowering yourself to be a part of petty arguments or disagreements. Your energy is too important for this; it needs to be kept high and not tainted by fear. Of course our personality has a hard time with this aspect of staying on the straight and narrow, and hence working with your Angelic guide will involve you making some wise decisions for your life.

Your Angelic guide can be contacted in the same way as your spirit guide. We each have an Angelic guide assigned to us and they'll come in when called. If you feel you're ready to go to the next level and work with your Angelic guide then ask your spirit guide for assistance in introducing you.

You can literally ask for this to happen, as you would any conversation with a friend. Simply ask to be introduced by your spirit guide, or if you feel confident to do so, call in your Angelic guide on your own. Your Angelic guide can give you a name to call them by, if it makes it easier for you to connect with them – just ask.

Once your Angelic guide becomes active in your life, get set for your spiritual growth to accelerate. You'll be privy to cosmic information you can use to master the universal forces. Remember that once you align with the Angelics, your own sense of deep self-responsibility will kick in. This happens naturally when we align with any energy that is of a higher vibration than our own.

You may also feel called to drop habits that lower your vibration and connection to source. For example, back in the mid-1990s, at the very beginning of my spiritual awakening, I felt the need to become vegetarian. At the time I did this because I loved animals and felt guilty about eating them, so I decided that I needed to be in alignment with my values.

As I've woken up over the ensuing years, I've become vegan and I just love the flow-on benefits it has brought to my body and to my spiritual skills. I'm sure that the Angelics had a hand in this decision, as embracing a plant-based diet has made my connection to them so much stronger.

Then, when my work with the Angelics began ramping up in the 2000s, I had the distinct call to stop drinking coffee. Not that there's anything wrong with coffee, but for me it felt as if drinking it daily was making my body dirty and heavy. Giving up coffee has made me physically appear lighter and younger. I've also noticed great acceleration in my healing work.

The Angelics know what's good for us, and if you follow their suggestions and lead, you truly will feel an equilibrium and satisfaction come into your physical life.

Past and future lives

We've spoken about the dimensions, the soul and the personality, spirit guides and the Angelic Realm; now let's look at our past and future life experiences. As a soul and an energetic light being, your very nature is eternal. You can transform and morph into varying shapes and forms at will. All choice truly is with you.

Yet once you commit to a human life, it's understood that you'll see it through until the moment comes when circumstances are aligned for you to go back home to spirit and leave your body behind.

Perhaps you already have an inkling that you've lived on Earth before, and perhaps you even have flashes of memory from these times. From the perspective of soul, keep in mind that we can incarnate into any form we wish, so human lives are not our only option.

As I explained in Chapter 3, our soul is like a great recorder of experiences. Every experience you've ever encountered becomes encoded upon the fabric of your soul, and can be tapped into for reference (and use) at any moment. The skills and talents that seem to come naturally to us have actually been learned over lifetimes.

The more we practise doing something, the better we become at it and the easier it becomes. So consider that you came into this lifetime with a whole set of unique life skills that were just waiting for you to tap into them and use them. Once we activate our natural talents and skills we also accelerate our life purpose.

Non-consecutive lives

Also consider that, from the perspective of the soul, lifetimes don't need to run in a consecutive fashion. I learned this first-hand one day while conducting a live guided meditation. I was teaching a past life course and was taking the group through a meditation to connect with a lifetime that was important to the one we were living today.

As I often do in my meditations, I was living the scene at the same time I was talking it through for everyone. My scene looked like Ancient Egypt. I was there as a female in a small temple with a group of others, and we were conducting what felt like a light ritual of some kind. This wasn't unusual for me, as I often saw myself in what felt like Ancient Egypt, conducting ceremony.

Then I guided everyone to enquire as to the timeframe they were in. When I did the same, I was shocked. I heard the year 2370. My personality started questioning this right away because we were in 2008 at the time. But then my soul rose up and allowed me to stop questioning.

I was looking into a scene on a *future* life, rather than a past life. I had heard of future lives before, but had never consciously experienced one. I also heard that I wasn't in Egypt but in a technologically advanced and spiritually aware society. It made me so excited to witness this, and also quite blown away that often what we feel is a past life could indeed be a glance into a future that soul is creating for us today.

Also consider that you can have breaks in between lives. We rarely incarnate straight into a new lifetime once our current one ends. We need space to integrate fully back home into spirit and consider all we've learned from our experiences. As souls, we like to meet up with our soul family and assess our progress with our teachers in spirit and our Angelic guides. Homecomings are always occasions for reflection and assimilation. We instinctively understand the need for rest and stillness.

Expanding your cosmic awareness

There are two powerful ways in which you can expand your awareness of the cosmos, and I'll share these with you now.

Meditation

The first way is to practise and experience meditation. Often when we hear the word 'meditation' it strikes up a fear or resistance within us, as if this is something that will slow us down, dumb us down, set us back or make us ungrounded. Yet meditation is far from this – in fact, it's one of the smartest, yet simplest, practices you can establish in your life. (See the two meditation practices in Chapter 1.)

When we meditate we simply shift focus on dimensions. This sounds very cosmic, doesn't it? As energy beings, we direct our attention at will. During daylight hours we tend to be focused on running the business of our everyday life, which puts our attention squarely in the physical dimension (for the most part). We may have fleeting moments where something causes us to pause and reflect, but this tends to be a minority experience for most people.

As someone who is now viewing themselves as a cosmic citizen and a growing Cosmic Messenger, I suggest that you start to make meditation a part of your daily lifestyle routine. Meditation helps us to grow spiritually and physically, as we consciously connect with our home base, our guides and our inner wisdom.

When we meditate we access slower brainwave states, much as we do when we sleep. This instantly shifts our vibration to trigger a healing response within the body. Meditation is fantastic for your health as well, as it lowers blood pressure and feeds your cells with light.

Out-of-body experiences (OBEs)

The second way to expand our cosmic awareness is via the out-of-body experience. Back in the mid-1990s, when I was first waking up, it was during my sleeping hours that the cosmos started making itself known to me.

As I explained in the Introduction to this book, I started having very vivid, *real-seeming* dream experiences every night. These experiences led me to trust in my multidimensional soul, as I felt myself move out of my body and travel as a light being through portals in space.

When I was out of my body I had no care for my physical presence back in my bed; I was free and I was also still me. I've never forgotten the first time this happened. I've since come to learn that when we sleep, we naturally meditate. Sleep shuts down our personality, as our body rests and our soul gets to take over. Just think of it: every night you have an opportunity for soul to be in charge and lead your life ahead. Beautiful, isn't it!?

Consider that as a soul made of energy you're able to move in and out of your physical body at will. Have you ever been daydreaming when someone interrupted you? Did you feel yourself jerk back into your body? What about when you're drifting off to sleep and a sound arouses you awake and you get the sensation of nearly falling out of your chair or the bed you're in?

I invite you to consider that soul can and does venture out of your body regularly. Most of the time we're not aware of this (consciously) because we're either asleep or in a state of deep meditation. Yet such out-of-body experiences, or OBEs, are commonplace.

Lucid dreaming

Let's look at your dream experiences, as this is how most people tend to have OBEs. One of the precursors to an OBE is lucid dreaming. Lucid dreaming happens when we become aware in our dream that we're dreaming. Has this ever happened to you? Perhaps you think you've woken up and try to turn on your bedside lamp, for example, but it melts in your hand? This is a conscious trigger that sparks an awareness that you're somewhere beyond the physical dimension.

When we become aware that we're dreaming it can evoke fear of the unknown, and at first it can scare us awake and out of the dream state. It does take practice to remain in lucid dreaming mode.

Yet the more you can try and remind yourself when you do wake up in a dream that it's OK and you're safe, the easier it'll be to sustain yourself in a lucid dream state. Why would you want to do this? Well, because once we're comfortable and skilled at lucid dreaming, the next stage in our spiritual development is the conscious out-of-body experience.

Sleep paralysis

A dreamtime OBE can come on after you've been lucid dreaming. Perhaps you can usually wake yourself up after a lucid episode, yet when an OBE develops it's harder to do this. You may experience sleep paralysis at first. This is the feeling (while asleep) that you consciously want to move, but your body just can't. It can feel like you're trapped in your body and can't get out.

Has this ever happened to you? This feeling tends to evoke fear in us, because no one likes the feeling of being paralysed and physically vulnerable. It's the fear that can then snap us back into our waking reality. You might wake up in bed after one of these episodes with a very heavy body and wonder what happened.

Again, the more you experience this state during sleep, the more you'll get used to it, and the fear will dissipate over time and with practice. It took several years of these night-time experiences before I had the courage to give over to my first conscious OBE. Once you're used to lucid dreaming and sleep paralysis, you may start to notice that your senses become heightened while asleep. Sounds, in particular, become vivid.

I can remember hearing what sounded like bees buzzing in my ears and knives slashing in my kitchen when I'd wake up seemingly paralysed at night. Yes, again this can evoke fear of the unknown and the extraordinary. As I explained earlier, when this happened to me repeatedly, I gave myself over to it and asked my soul, *Is this good for me?* I heard 'yes'. When I gave into the high-vibration sounds (instead of resisting them) the noises subsided and I relaxed.

What happens during an OBE?

My body can literally buzz when I'm about to have an OBE. It's as if every atom of my being moves at high speed, all at once. It can seem very noisy too, almost like a rotary lawnmower on full power. I've come to learn that this is the sound of soul moving out of the body and travelling between dimensions.

If you can let yourself go and trust that what is happening is for your higher good, it can seem like you're dunked under water for a moment, almost as if your breath is taken away. But then you emerge through what I can only describe as a tunnel of light, moving at warp speed through the dark cosmos.

I love this part of having an OBE and travelling to other dimensions. It feels like I'm on a galactic roller-coaster. I can sense excitement for where I'm going. It's as if my soul has its own GPS and knows exactly where our destination lies.

Now, not everyone will experience the same sensations as I do during a night-time OBE. It depends on your belief systems. I've found that the more open-minded we are, the more vivid and well rounded our experiences tend to be.

One frequent dream sign that helps me to know when an OBE is coming on after a lucid dream is seeing animals, especially cats in front of doors or windows. It's as though they are gatekeepers and way showers into other worlds. I love it when I see this symbol, as I know I will have a safe and inspired journey with my animal guide by my side.

Indeed, you can have some unsavoury experiences during OBEs. In my experience there are some heavy energy fields around Earth and it takes some practice to navigate through them. You may have heard of the 'Astral Belt' around Earth. This is a space I'm familiar with and yes, it does contain beings (remember there are many different life forms in our cosmos) that thrive on fear-based thoughts.

I tend to find that those humans who are overdoing drugs or alcohol or are locked into mental dire straits tend to dance around this field. As you're passing through the astral on your way out and into the cosmos, you can get pulled back by these beings and get almost stuck in this realm for a bit.

It can become seductive in that souls out of their body manifest themselves in any way they choose and many love to have astral sexual encounters. If you've heard of astral sex, well, it does exist. If you find yourself stuck in this realm, simply ask your spirit guide or Angelic guide to come in and help you through. They will hear you. It simply takes practice to remember to do this.

Once you become quite adept at moving through the astral realm, you can bypass it altogether and enjoy conscious OBE trips to other higher realms and dimensions. The best way to achieve this is to keep your body clear and clean before sleep and hold the intention of travelling protected and for your highest good.

If you're wondering how your soul knows the way back to your physical body after you've had an OBE, trust me, it does. I've felt the cord that many speak of – it's like an etheric lifeline between soul and the body, almost like those lines astronauts use during spacewalks – which snaps us back in each time. When you wake up from an OBE your body may be overtly aware of its heaviness and you can feel groggy and ungrounded the next day.

It's my understanding that upon our physical death we have a permanent OBE. The cord that attaches us to our physical body is released and soul automatically zips us back to home base, without any hitches along the way. You'll also be assisted by your spirit guide to ensure you have a safe and enjoyable trip back home.

You've probably heard or read countless personal accounts of near-death experiences. I encourage you to do your own research about OBEs. I trust that my experiences may be similar to yours and that they can give you some point of reference to work with and springboard from.

CHAPTER 8

Momentum and Resistance

B ack in Chapter 4 we explored the importance of engaging our imagination in order to become a visionary as we accelerate our life purpose. Once you're using your imagination – and soul is giving you strong desires that you're acting on (desires that'll see you fulfil your life purpose) – you'll start to notice an interesting chain of events.

Momentum and moving ahead

Whenever we start to move ahead we create a forward force called *momentum*. Momentum is a natural occurrence in the physical dimension, once you take *action*. Without action, momentum doesn't exist and you won't see yourself progress.

As I said in Chapter 5, it's *action that accelerates your life purpose*. Now, given that the physical reality is a divided one and that everything on Earth is experienced through the lens of duality, momentum creates an equal (yet opposite) force at the same time as we move ahead.

Have you ever started something new and felt a great rush of excitement as you did so? It's as if you're on a slipstream of energy and are easily accelerating. Then something happens and you get stopped. It could be that your plans change, or someone criticizes what you're doing, or your excitement turns into uncertainty, or you feel unsure – and then basically, self-doubt creeps in. Why does this happen? Why is it that every time we think we're on a roll, something or someone comes in to disrupt that flow?

Resistance is good for you

Well, just as the force of momentum moves you ahead in the physical dimension, its equal opposite force, *resistance*, also moves you back. Momentum is the positive pole and resistance is its negative. Every action that we take creates an equal and opposite reaction. This is nature's law because in order to be in unity and wholeness (like our mirror, the spiritual dimension), the physical dimension breaks down all phenomena into two equal halves.

Our physical life is a divided dimension of experiences, as I explained when we spoke about the soul in Chapter 2. When you acknowledge that the two halves make one whole, then you're in balance or unity.

UNIVERSAL SECRET 8:

'Resistance is the other half of momentum.'

Every experience we have is divided into two, which is why sadness accompanies joy and dark accompanies light. The two energies make up one whole, and as curious souls (which we are) we love to dissect the universe into its parts so we can study them and truly understand what makes a united reality tick.

The two energies combine as one. You can't have momentum without resistance. You can't move ahead without an equal and opposite force also pushing you back. It's the resistance that gives you strength. Quite literally, it's resistance that propels a plane into the air. It takes a lot of thrust and momentum for the plane to lift off and it's the force moving against the forward movement that allows it to rise. You're just like that plane. Without resistance pushing against your forward momentum, *you* wouldn't be able to fly.

Resistance is meant to happen

Often when we experience some form of resistance our initial reaction is one of annoyance or even fear. Imagine this: you've finally got a clear idea of which steps you need to take to enact your life purpose and you begin walking your talk. The first few days or even weeks can seem elevating. You're on a roll, optimistic and feeling good about the future you're creating.

Then suddenly (seemingly out of the blue) you experience what might seem like a roadblock. That forward momentum you've been creating appears to stop and in its place a whole set of questions and/or doubts start creeping in. Does this sound familiar? Do you wonder why every time you move ahead something happens to pull you back?

Resistance is good for you; it's meant to happen. Resistance makes you stronger, wiser and accomplished. Resistance causes us to improve upon what it is we're creating, especially when it comes to our life purpose. Understanding how momentum and resistance work hand in hand accelerates your life purpose.

Whenever you're moving ahead you'll create resistance in response to your momentum. This is a normal part of human life. There's nothing wrong with resistance. Momentum isn't better than resistance; they're simply two parts of one whole: the negative and positive, the dark and the light. Both are needed and both exist in the spiritual dimension. Mastery of resistance and momentum is down to how you accept challenges and how you work them to your advantage.

For example, while I was writing this particular chapter I kept getting stopped. It wasn't because I didn't know what I wanted to write, because I did and I was actually keen to explain how momentum and resistance work together. Instead I was experiencing resistance to my momentum, at the same time that I was writing about it.

Knowing how the universe works, I actually found this quite humorous. The constant urge to get up and walk around and check my social media and e-mails was distracting me. Now if I hadn't known that this resistance was a normal response to my enthusiastic momentum, I might have stopped and considered that I wasn't meant to be writing this chapter, or the book. Can you imagine that? This book would never have come about. This is a perfect example of what stops so many people from fulfilling their dreams and life purpose.

By coming to recognize what resistance is and how it works in tandem with momentum, you can relieve your self-doubt. Remember that resistance is a good sign, as it implies that you're moving ahead. Once you accept and come to expect resistance as a *by-product* of momentum, your insecurities will have the opportunity to fade away and be replaced by your inner excitement and a keener focus and awareness on your important tasks at hand.

You can now see why some people never get their projects off the ground and build the valuable momentum they need. It's simply because they're afraid of the resistance. Perhaps this has happened to you in the past, or maybe it's happening right now? It certainly used to happen to me. I can remember during the years before I woke up, I was convinced that good things wouldn't last (momentum) and that bad things always happened (resistance). With the level of consciousness I had at the time, that was my summation of how life worked. Perhaps you can relate to this?

I've since come to learn from study and first-hand experience that good (positive) and bad (negative) things do go hand in hand and that the more I focus on moving ahead, using my resistance to help me fly, the greater my rewards and life satisfaction become.

✷ PRACTICE ✷
Embrace your resistance

Just as you would go to a gym to improve your muscle tone and bone strength by lifting weights and doing *resistance* work, you can also work out your life purpose in the same way. The next time you encounter resistance to your forward momentum, try the following exercise:

1. When you feel resistance coming towards you – i.e. you keep getting distracted from what you're creating or life isn't flowing uninterrupted – *stop*. Rather than pushing through at all costs, consider that you're being sent a message by soul.

2. Recognize that *your momentum* is creating the resistance. Give yourself credit for this. Even if it seems as if someone or something else is pushing against you and stopping you from moving ahead, remind yourself that it's your forward force creating this backwards energy.

3. Tell yourself, 'This is a good sign.' Notice how this makes you feel – are you now lighter, released, more energized and ready to go again?

4. After a pause to gather your thoughts and centre yourself, start to take further positive action steps in the direction of your dreams, projects and purpose. Try not to wait too long to do this. Resistance isn't meant to stop you for days or weeks. A few minutes, hours or perhaps a day should be plenty of time. Don't lose the valuable momentum you've already created.

5. Simply go back and recommence what you were moving ahead with. You'll find that you have a different perspective to the one you had before the resistance arose. See how much extra energy you have as well. Remind yourself that resistance helps to make you stronger and more informed. You'll then be well on your way to manifesting your desires and accelerating your life purpose.

Complacency keeps you stuck

It's important that you don't wait too long to recommence building momentum once resistance arises. In fact, you could experience the resistance and still keep moving, depending on its strength. It takes an enormous amount of will and energy production on your part to produce momentum.

To keep your personality on track, knowing that it's doing the work of your soul, it's key not to let resistance get the better of you. Go easy on yourself at first. You'll get the hang of it and be given lots of situations in which to practice.

What can be deflating (more than anything else) is *complacency*. *Complacency serves to keep you stuck.* Just like momentum, complacency is also self-generated. The opposite energy force to complacency is *enthusiasm*. The more you can generate enthusiasm about what you're involved with, the less likely it is that complacency will take a hold of your life.

Try and recall a recent situation in which you allowed complacency to take over. Did you lose your focus, were you tired and worn out or did you just become a little too comfortable with your status quo? It's easy to become complacent, especially when you're on a mission and feel as though you're constantly striving towards a life purpose goal with no let-up in sight.

Often we can put the brakes on our own projects and make ourselves become complacent (on purpose), in order to get a rest. Sound familiar? Do you forge ahead and then find you don't have the energy or desire to keep going? Perhaps you never give yourself a break as you're creating momentum and fielding resistance? If so, I urge you to consider that complacency can be your friend, especially if it's an energy that you often find yourself experiencing.

Being grateful

Sometimes we can be complacent more than we're enthusiastic, especially if we don't have a plan or a purpose for our life. Do you find it hard to generate enthusiasm for what you're involved with? If this is the case, then one of the easiest ways I've found to shift complacency is to *be grateful*. When the daily grind of life gets to us, we can often forget to show and feel gratitude. Yet being grateful is so simple and it instantly lifts our energy to the level of enthusiasm, which meets and then neutralizes complacency.

How do you practise being grateful? Well, it's simple. While you're lying in bed at night and before you go to sleep, take a few moments to allow your mind to drift back through the day without judgement, as you just observe.

Then take a few deep breaths in and out and start to say 'thank you'. Start to say it for the simple things. You can say 'thank you' for the warm bed you're in, the roof over your head, the running water in your taps, the electricity that powers your home, your friends and family, your animals, or the Sun that gives you life. *Choose something that has meaning to you.*

This little practice takes just a few minutes but it's surprisingly effective. It will feed and nourish your energy field and connect you with soul and the spiritual dimension, lifting your enthusiasm in the most elegant and grounded way.

You can also practise being grateful while stuck in traffic in your car, while sitting on the bus, or on a plane or train. *Gratitude moves complacency quickly* and allows you to come to a place where soul can be heard and your deepest desires tapped into directing your life purpose.

Working through self-doubt

One of the biggest challenges for most of us is working through our self-generated doubt. To varying degrees, we all have doubts about our abilities and potential. These can be triggered by outside events, other people, cosmic energy, our own expectations, and of course by the resistance that we generate when we do decide to move ahead.

Self-doubt can show up in many different forms and guises. It can manifest as negative inner talk, which comes from the personality feeling all alone and disconnected from soul. Go back into Chapter 2 if you need assistance with this. Self-doubt can also be triggered by past life memories, by people pointing out what we consider to be our faults, by the breakdown of important relationships and by having perhaps unrealistic timeframes and ideals for our life purpose.

Doubt can cripple us. Yet when we look at the opposite energy to self-doubt (in this divided universe of form) we find *confidence* or *self-confidence*. Do you consider yourself to be a confident person or someone who often self-doubts? Perhaps you experience a mix of the two, depending on the situation? What if you considered that confidence simply comes from trusting in your abilities?

In fact, confidence is a learned skill that comes from putting yourself on the line each day and proving your skills and abilities by using them, and by putting yourself to the test. One of the best ways I know to prove our worth and gain confidence is to be *responsible*.

Responsibility and Freedom

One night back in 2004, I went through a very intense out-of-body experience. I had been to a spiritual class earlier in the evening and was feeling on a high. When I went to sleep I had a feeling that I was going to be exploring in my sleep. Sure enough, at about 3 a.m. I felt myself wake up within my dream and I started to have a conscious OBE. (See Chapter 7 to learn more about the out-of-body experience process.)

While I was out travelling through other dimensions, I can clearly remember being shown an equation on what looked like a space wall. By space wall, I mean I was hovering in space looking out into the dark with distant stars all around me, as a giant equation started forming in front of me. It looked as if it was being written on an invisible wall in space.

This equation was illuminated by white light and I was mesmerized by it. I'll never forget what it said. I instinctively knew that it was a message from soul and my guides that would have great life purpose meaning for me. The message was:

RESPONSIBILITY = FREEDOM

At the time *freedom* was one of the values I held most dear. I was actively on my path, and building up my business so I could be entirely self-employed as my own boss and support myself in my desired holistic lifestyle.

I was constantly wondering where and how freedom came into this scenario – it was something that I focused on every day.

When I saw that responsibility gives rise to freedom it confused me at first. Perhaps it does you, too? How can responsibility – which infers work and focus and perhaps even sacrifice – equate to freedom?

Well, I'll tell you how. *There's nothing more empowering than knowing what you're capable of.* And I don't mean just thinking about your capabilities – I mean actually using them and proving them to yourself by generating your own first-hand experience.

Now this is where *responsibility* comes in. The more responsible you become, the more you tend to extend your talents and skills into the world around you. This means you'll be using your natural abilities more often. Rather than sitting back and letting someone else take the reins of your life, you'll step up and do so, especially when it's your job (and your responsibility).

The more responsible you become, the more you know what you're capable of, and this, dear friend, is what frees you. As you step up and learn how to work through life's challenges, the less hold they have over you, and thus you experience a freedom that is quite divine.

There's perhaps nothing more crippling than having to rely solely on someone or something else to support you. Have you ever known someone who can't do anything for themselves – not because they're incapable, but because they choose not to? Is that person free or are they imprisoned by their own inability to know how capable they are?

I invite you to test out the accuracy of this statement for yourself. Responsibility = Freedom? Try it, Cosmic Messenger, and you shall know.

CHAPTER 9

Noticing the Signs

As I explained earlier, as a soul living a human life you have natural, universal abilities that are just waiting to be tapped into and used. One of these abilities is the skill of *manifestation*. Whether you realize it or not, you're applying your mind to create what it is you experience from moment to moment.

You are a natural manifestor

Mind is a field of thoughts that is generated by your applied thinking. The entire universe operates within a mind field, for as souls this is how we communicate with one another and interact with all living beings. It's your heart (soul) that generates ideas within the field of mind and sends them to your personality (head) for processing and to begin the action part of manifestation.

So what is manifestation? Well, you could consider manifestation as the physical outcropping of your ideas. To manifest means to *make real* and to bring forward from the invisible dimension to the visible dimension, from spirit into physicality.

When you were conceived, you began to manifest into form. The idea of *you* began to take on physical measure and started unfolding within your mother's womb. This process of manifestation from soul to human form took *action* on the part of yourself and your parents. For indeed, taking action is a critical step in manifestation.

I invite you to consider that *manifesting* is as natural to you as breathing. You really don't need to think about it and it happens. Yet this is the important factor – when you *do* place some consideration (thought) into what you desire to manifest, this is when the magic starts to happen in your life and your purpose begins to take on greater meaning and depth.

As a natural manifestor it's vital that you reclaim this power in a conscious way and use it for your highest good. Directing your desires and knowing what it is you wish to create help you to achieve your life goals in an easier and faster form.

The process of manifestation

Let's break down the process of manifestation, so that you can see where your attention is required in order to manifest with awareness. Manifestation begins within your soul and by the generation of your soul's desires. In Chapter 2 I discussed the differences between soul and personality. Reread that chapter now if you need a refresh on this.

Soul knows why we're here and what we desire to learn this lifetime. All of this information is recorded upon your soul and can be tapped into and unlocked once your personality decides to take direction from the heart.

Your desire

In the process of manifestation soul firstly comes up with a desire. Let's say it's important for you to acquire your own home. Soul starts sending messages and images to the head (the personality) of you living in your own space, and being happy and content and fulfilled there. You start receiving recurring images that activate your longing to have a home of your own.

Actioning your desire

Once your personality keeps receiving these messages, it's time to do something about making this desire happen. It's your personality's task to action the desires of soul (the heart).

So in our example of owning a home, you may start looking online at properties. Your finances will call to be looked at, so you may decide to start saving more and spending less. You might want to earn a higher salary and so start looking at a shift in career or perhaps furthering your education. You may look at where you can cut back and what you can let go of in order to bring your desire of owning your own home closer to manifestation.

Whatever steps you feel drawn to take, take them. This is how we manifest our ideas into physical reality – and it's how we manifest a sense of accomplishment. When you're aware of what you're consciously creating, accomplishment naturally builds.

The more aware you are of what it is you're consciously creating, the easier it becomes to manifest your desires. Energy follows our direct intent. Therefore, the more that you can focus on what it is you're creating, the sooner it manifests. This is because your full power is behind it. *It's your natural ability to manifest.* All you're required to do is remember how to use this ability – by using it often!

UNIVERSAL SECRET 9:

'The universe responds to your call once you start taking action towards what you desire.'

Once you begin to *action* your desires, and you then start seeing signs of manifestation, it's your recognition of this that triggers something quite special. Your recognition of what you're manifesting sends out an instant call to the universe to put its full cosmic weight behind your creation.

When the universe does this, your manifestations rapidly advance. You then receive cosmic help from your spirit guides, the Angelics, and the cosmic field of mind of which you're a part.

It's not enough just to *think* about what it is you wish to create, you need to *do* something about making it happen as well. It's your action that the universe waits for. So if you're wondering why your manifestations don't come about, or they happen haphazardly, or if you think that the universe isn't on your side, then reconsider. Are you actually letting yourself down by not following through on your ideas? Are you giving up too soon, before the universe even has a chance to respond?

Keep in mind that universal time will work differently to your own personal clock. Once the universal forces come in and support your manifestations, a whole raft of higher-level life scenarios start to form. You may not be seeing the bigger picture that the universe has in mind for you, and that's where trust comes in, as you turn your focus to noticing the signs that you're being helped.

Reading energy, and your energy field

Once you begin to accept that you're a natural manifestor – by taking action on your desires and becoming aware that cosmic forces are assisting you – it becomes imperative that you can also *read energy*.

In Chapter 1, we began our exploration of the cosmos by looking at energy and the role it plays in our life. Everything is made of energy and as energy beings we're actually adept energy readers. As with manifestation, reading energy is a natural skill that we possess. We simply need to rediscover our talent for reading energy, as we acknowledge it and then use it often.

From moment to moment we're making internal decisions based upon our ability to read energy. In Chapter 1 I discussed how we can sense energy through mindful awareness. We sense energy first on a subtle or invisible level. We have an energy field (or aura) that extends beyond our body, and it's through this field, which is generated by the vibration and movement of our body's major energy centres, that we communicate with the universe around us.

Your energy field is an individual expression and also part of the cosmic energy field. It's through your energy field that you pick up on vibration and decide if you meet an energy match or mismatch to your natural flow. Therefore, you're constantly interacting with others and making assumptions and/or decisions based on the subtle clues that you pick up through your energy field.

For example, you can read when someone or something does or doesn't resonate with you. Your stomach may churn or you might feel the need to step back if you're out of alignment with the person or the situation. Likewise, you may feel your body bubbling with excitement and warmth around the heart when you encounter someone or something that *does* resonate with your energy.

When the universe comes in to assist with your manifestation it's important to start noticing the energy readings and feedback you're picking up from anything related to what it is you're manifesting. Listen to your body's call, for your body is directly responding to energy and helping you to read subtle messages.

When you pick up on an instinctive energy message, recognize it. Stop and pay attention to what you're feeling. Make it real by *giving it your focus*. This is what allows you to make productive decisions based on the energy you're reading from situations.

Once you become practised at reading energy and trust in what you pick up on, then you'll start to notice your *repetitive personal signs*. These are the signs that are unique to you. They will offer further assistance in determining the next steps to take with your manifestation.

✴ PRACTICE ✴
Identify your personal signs

Personal signs are unique indicators that trigger a 'yes' or 'no' response within you. You may already have some personal signs that you've used and relied upon for most of your life. Perhaps you know them well?

- Do you have a favourite number? If so, what does it mean to you when you see it, particularly if you see it when you're thinking about or taking action towards what you wish to manifest?

- Is there a particular song that holds a positive meaning for you? What happens when you hear it?

- Are there signs in nature that trigger a response of powerful meaning within you – like a feather falling, a bird singing, the wind blowing, the rain trickling, a rainbow appearing or the Sun breaking through clouds? I often notice car horns beeping, dogs barking or bells ringing just after I've made a statement that *rings true* for me. It's one of my personal 'yes' signs.

- Start taking note of personal signs that come to you, particularly when you're in the middle of a conversation, deep in thought or actively pursuing your dreams.

- Record your signs in writing, so you become very aware of what they are and what they mean to you. In this way you'll be conscious of your signs when they appear. You'll then take good note of what the universe is telling you, because the universe speaks to us and directs us through our personal signs.

Working with synchronicity and signs

Knowing that the cosmic forces, including your spirit guide and Angelic team, are working with you by sending personal signs, is a comforting experience. It shows you that the entire universe is coming together and orchestrating with you the outcomes and results that will see your desires manifest as your life purpose is met.

It's a real buzz to receive a sign, isn't it? It can make your body tingle, as your vibration meets the exacting vibration of what it is you're manifesting. What's even more powerful, and indicates that you're forging ahead, is when you receive a series of signs in sequence.

This is *synchronicity* and it shows how much influence we wield upon the universal mind field. When a series of events takes place that is too uncanny to dismiss, we're jolted awake and almost forced to sit up and take notice. The signs come in at a rapid rate and confirm to us that we're on the right path – or that we need to change, and do so pronto.

Positive and negative signs

How will you know if a sign or synchronicity is positive or negative towards your cause? Well, it all has to do with the feelings and feedback mechanisms your body sends you as you receive the sign or synchronous series of events.

Back in late October 2005 I was travelling around the globe visiting many ancient monuments and power places and had a desire to go to India. I was in Egypt at the time and was planning my next stop. But every travel agent I went to had an issue with flights. They were either unavailable on the dates I wanted or the cost was too high. I then went to the Indian embassy to get a visa and it was closed and wouldn't be open for another four days.

After spending five hours on a hot day in crowded Cairo noticing the repetitive personal signs and synchronicity, I took stock and decided it wasn't the right time to visit India. This was a good decision, as only a week later (which is just as I'd have been arriving) there was a series of major bombings in Delhi, where I had been planning to head.

I listened to my signs and missed being in probable danger. I also booked a trip to Jordan instead and had the most soul-enhancing experience – travelling to Petra and immersing myself in the ancient Nabataean culture. It was a good decision on my part. I'm glad I noticed, listened to and followed my signs.

Can you look back at a time in your life when you noticed the signs and rather than ignoring them, listened to them and followed their cues? Did you have a good outcome? What about the times when you ignored synchronicity and went ahead anyway? Did you end up having regrets or have to go through a situation that was a hard life lesson?

When we work with the signs and synchronicity, life flows beautifully. We become aware that we're in constant communion with the universe and everything that happens to us is a co-creation with the divine. The more you act upon your signs, the more you show your trust in spirit and your personality begins to trust in soul. It can be fun to watch out for your signs and quite a magical experience too. It brings back our childlike sense of awe and appreciation for the web of life.

Working with your signs is vital for powerful manifesting. It ensures we use our awareness to create situations of positivity that will enhance our human experience, rather than moving through each day unaware and inadvertently manifesting situations and events we don't consciously desire.

Double and triple digit and master number sequences

Another way in which the spiritual dimension, soul and the cosmos communicate with us is through sending signs by means of double and/or triple number sequences. Have you ever seen the numbers 11:11 for example? This double-digit sequence (and master number in numerology) has become something of a hallmark of spiritual awakening and the opening of a gateway of opportunity.

The study of numbers is quite fascinating. Numbers truly do form the basis of our cosmic universe, and every structure and form in nature can be explained with numbers. I can remember during an OBE one night in 2004, being taken into space and shown how the universe and the mind field is represented by mathematical equations.

At the time my soul was so excited, I was sure I'd remember the number sequences I was shown when I woke up. Alas, I couldn't remember a thing (which is often the case), but I could rest assured that my soul had taken notes and that what I needed to know would assist me in my life purpose going forward.

Master numbers in numerology are numbers that contain double digits, such as 11, 22, 33, 44, 55, 66, 77, 88 and 99. These double numbers magnify the power of the single digit incredibly. When we see or are given a master number to work with it can often indicate that we're coming into a *masterful stage* in our life, one of greater responsibility and therefore greater possible reward.

Some people are born with master numbers in their birth date or name, making their life path one that requires particular discipline. Most of us will manifest signs of master number sequences as we evolve in life, particularly during periods of cosmic energy shifts and profound or rapid expansion.

Master numbers and double and triple digits often arise in our life when *we're in the cosmic flow*. They are congratulatory indicators that we're following our signs and manifesting with ease. When you see one, close your eyes and say 'thank you'. This recognition is an honouring and receiving of the cosmic abundance now coming your way.

Interpreting number sequences

Below are my interpretations of master numbers and common double and triple number sequences:

11: New beginnings abound. Opportunities are here. You're accelerating.

22: You're in a peaceful flow. Practical groundwork is being laid. Partnerships.

33: Spiritual and cosmic responsibility calls. Be a peacemaker. Social expansion.

44: The Angelic Realm works through you. You're walking your talk.

55: Rapid change and expansion are imminent. Travel and freedom call.

66: Harmonious relationships are key. Family and nostalgia lead the way.

77: The spiritual teacher in you rises. Study and reflection are called for.

88: Abundant expansion is imminent. Powerful energy. Balance is required.

99: Completion and artistic expression call. Wisdom comes through endings.

11:11: Gateways of opportunity have opened. You're moving ahead.

2:22: You're working well in partnership. Continue with teamwork.

3:33: The cosmic energy flows through you. Self-doubt is possible.

4:44: The Angelic Realm calls you to world service. You're a messenger.

5:55: You're a conduit for change. Be spontaneous and flexible.

CHAPTER 10

The Power of Secrecy

W e now come to one of the most important of the Universal Secrets that will facilitate the conscious evolution of your life purpose. Perhaps more than any other secret, this is the one that seals the success of your dreams and ensures they're put into motion. What we desire and what is born of soul and arises from our heart is precious to us.

Your desires are precious

We each have individual desires that are sacred to who we are and our incredible life path. No one else has ever had quite the same desires as you have, because no one else has followed quite the same life path as yours. Therefore, consider that what soul desires for your life is *personal to you.*

Whenever we come across something that we consider precious, our natural instinct is to hold it close and look after it. We place value upon what is precious, and so I'd ask you to start doing this with your desires for your life. Rather than dismissing your dreams as far-fetched, start embracing them as real and possible manifestations. If any semblance of self-doubt arises when you consider fulfilling your desires, catch it in the act as you raise your awareness. You're the *gatekeeper to your desires coming true.*

One of the first steps in making this happen is to *honour* what you would love to create for yourself. Hold one of your precious desires in your mind's eye right now. Use your imagination to paint a picture of what you look, sound and feel like when you're actually living this desire.

Can you see this desire coming true? Can you see it as a real possibility for your life? Manifestation begins when you nurture your desires by building them up in your imagination first and foremost.

Manifesting what you desire

In Chapter 9 we spoke about the steps to take when manifesting our desires. Have a reread if you need to go over these again. You'll remember that once we've built up an idea of what we desire (via our imagination) we then need to take action steps towards our desire becoming a reality. This is when the universe steps in to assist us: *at the action part.*

It's your forward movement and momentum that give the cosmos the go-ahead to come in and help you. This then brings us to an important step in the manifestation process – one we haven't yet spoken about.

UNIVERSAL SECRET 10:
'Secrecy builds incredible power.'

Whenever you're creating something new and manifesting a desire that is entirely precious and personal to you, it's vital that you *keep it secret*. Now I'm not suggesting that you lie about what you desire. What I *am* saying is that you keep it to yourself, especially in the beginning stages, as your desire is being born.

When a couple becomes pregnant, they tend not to tell others the news until the baby is well along, usually into the third month. At this stage, it's safe to say that all is travelling well within the pregnancy and revealing the news won't risk the manifestation of the child. However, if you reveal your plans and dreams too early, it's possible that you'll attract the ire and negative attention of others, which can compromise your ability to manifest.

Perhaps you'll also attract a positive response if you reveal the news of what it is you're manifesting before it's got off the ground. However, at such an early stage you may not have 100 per cent confidence in what it is you're creating. There could be a small (or even large) seed of self-doubt within you. Now if you tell everyone about your plans and dreams before they've seeded, you run the risk of others' opinions triggering that *seed of self-doubt* that you hold. After all, everyone has an opinion when we're creating something new. Yes?

Remember in Chapter 8 I said that your forward motion (your momentum) will attract resistance and that resistance could show up in the form of others pushing against you? To alleviate any outside influences that could cause you to doubt and/or stop you from moving ahead with your desires, follow the ancient code of keeping your plans to yourself until they have had time to grow roots and gain a footing in the physical world.

Now if there are *one or two people* who have your best interests at heart and are not threatened by your success in any way, then by all means share your plans with them. This could be a very close friend, family member, partner, etc. Keep it close between you both and work on it together, if you like. Otherwise, work on your desires (yourself) in the quiet of your own making. The power of secrecy ensures that your desires manifest rather than fizzle out before they've even begun.

Keeping the energy tight

The major reason we keep our desires close to our chest while they're in their infancy is to *keep the energy tight*. What this means is that by not releasing your ideas, dreams and desires to the outside world, and *acting* on them instead, you create an enormous force behind them. Your momentum becomes so great that any resistance you self-create will simply push you higher.

So once you come up with a desire for your life, just start working towards it. There's no need to tell everyone what you're doing, why you're doing it and what you hope to gain from it. *Just do it instead.* We need to resist the temptation to share our plans and dreams before they've even begun to come true.

When I was first approached by Hay House to write this book, I knew straight away to keep the information tight. My personality may have wanted to tell people close to me about this exciting event, but my soul knew instinctively to employ the power of secrecy.

It wasn't until after my manuscript was finished that I felt I could begin to share my news publicly. This was because I had taken action, my book had manifested and it had gained so much momentum that its growth into adulthood was assured. This is how I run all of the projects in my life. I've learned simply to focus quietly on my work and then when it's ready to be released, the energy becomes so strong that it's guaranteed to be well received.

What personal desires do you currently have that you could keep tight? Are you actively working towards them or are you still in the imagining stage? I suggest you consider using *the power of secrecy* the next time you're about to create something special and important in your life. Talk it out with yourself and your guides, or if you need to, with someone very close to you. Then set about taking the daily action steps to make it happen. Resist the temptation to tell the world until you're ready to launch. Grow your momentum instead. Give yourself and your creations the best starting chance in life.

Following an ancient code

When we follow *the power of secrecy*, we're actually following an ancient code. The ancient ones (who were just like you) knew how to keep their information tight. Whether through a royal line, religious organizations, governments or secret groups and societies, doctrines and ways were quietly passed down from one generation to the next. By keeping information secure among only those who needed to know it, the longevity of the information was ensured.

The ancients would often even hide their information within codes that were only known to a select few. Again this was to ensure the outcropping of a desired manifestation. Now you may consider that keeping information secret from the world has done us a collective disservice. In many cases this is true, but what we're speaking about is manifesting your personal day-to-day desires.

Indeed, in the age of technology, with information being so freely shared, the power of secrecy perhaps needs a reboot. Rather than manipulating others by holding back what could help them, let's look at being more discerning about what it is we choose to share and/or seek to know.

Be discerning

Discernment is a life skill that is learned through experience. When you become discerning you choose for yourself *wisely*. In keeping your desires secret in their infancy, you're being discerning. You're giving yourself space to explore what it is you're creating, before the world comes in and tells you why you should or shouldn't be creating it.

See if the power of secrecy works for you by trying it out. There's so much we can learn from the ancient ones, and indeed from ourselves. Look back at your past failures and successes and ask yourself if using the power of secrecy would have helped you more or less? Determine how you'll now decide to manifest your most precious desires.

CHAPTER 11

Cultivating Your Uniqueness

In the entire memory of the universe there has only ever been one you. You're evolving from moment to moment. The being that you were just one second ago is different to the being that you are now. Just stop for a moment and consider this. Close your eyes and reflect upon your life's journey.

You are an original

See yourself as a child, then as a soul before you were born into this human life. Perhaps images emerge of past lifetimes on Earth or elsewhere? You've experienced so much and you continue to do so each day as you evolve and grow and add to the beauty and pattern of soul.

In cultivating our uniqueness it's important to realize just how *individual* we truly are. While we're all born of the same light, we each have a will and desire that shapes our form. The beauty of having your own, self-directed will is that you get to create yourself just the way you choose to. No one on high is telling you how to live your life – soul is choosing for you based upon your experiences.

When I was first beginning my holistic business back in 2000, I came up with a by-line because I felt it was important to express the meaning and energy behind the work I was offering. My by-line was and still is, *Experience Your Soul.* I knew instinctively that experience was everything to the soul and that if we could just feel (first-hand) what it's like to be a soul in a human body, it would help us to move onto our life purpose.

Can you see how your personal experiences mould your individuality? Are you often comparing yourself to others in an attempt to justify who you are, or perhaps to gauge how your progress is coming along?

Be your own role model

I invite you to consider something quite radical: start to see and treat yourself as an *original creation.* There's no comparison to you. Rather than looking to others for your lead, why not start leading yourself and decide to become *your own role model?* Be inspired by you. Be uplifted by you.

This takes practice, as it's the personality's habit to look outside of itself for inspiration. However, the more that you can focus on soul leading your life, and using yourself as the example, the easier it becomes to be self-ignited.

Universal Secret 11:
'You're the one you're looking for.'

The next time you feel the urge to check out what all of your friends, peers or idols are up to, stop and ask yourself, *Why am I doing this?* See what soul says to you and then shift your course.

Tell yourself, *I'm the role model. I'm the one who lives with excellence.* You're enough, just as you are. See your beauty. You're growing each day into the being that you choose to be. Notice how this viewpoint elegantly shifts your energy onto a high level of manifestation.

Pulling from your life experiences

Given that we're spiritual beings in human lives learning from our experiences, it follows that we can use those life experiences to great advantage. Each day, the way that we respond and interact with people and situations tends to be due to our automated stored cellular memory.

Every time we have an experience it's recorded upon the soul for reuse and re-examination, as and when we need it. Yet, what if you knew that your responses didn't have to be automatic and that you could make an in-the-moment choice?

When we stop to consider that we have a choice in how we respond to life, we can make *informed decisions*. Just imagine that, before responding to any situation, you can decide to create space and take a few moments to centre yourself and pull into soul. You just have to practise doing this *before* you're put on the spot. Make it a new daily habit to wait a few moments before responding to anyone or anything.

Even if you feel overwhelmed by the emotions triggered by circumstances you feel are out of your control, you still have a choice. When this happens, quickly imagine that you're snapping an invisible rubber band on your wrist to grab your attention.

Creating space in between you and your decision is powerful. When you do this you can consciously pull from your life experiences. You can decide in your power, rather than from a place of fear or uncertainty. As I said, this takes practice, so I suggest you start with small acts of power each day.

For example, if someone asks something of you out of the blue in a phone call, text or email, stop before you respond. Take a moment and decide what's in your best interests. If someone confronts you while you're out living your day, resist the urge to lash out. Again, take a moment and see how differently you choose to respond.

Sometimes just being quiet says it all. *When you're in stillness, you're in soul.* It only takes a moment of stillness to reset the busyness. When you give yourself that split second to consider your options, you'll be creating conscious (aware) experiences that can then become the automated responses of your future.

Stepping back from those who aren't in alignment with you

When you create the space *to think* in-between decisions you'll come to view yourself and others in a whole new light. So often we're simply responding to life automatically, without considering the consequences of our actions. This is what then causes regret about our past. All of this can be avoided (going forward) if we simply decide to become more astute Cosmic Messengers and readers of energy each day.

When you create space around a decision, you effectively move yourself out of the field of others in order to better gauge your true feelings and soul's direction. When you do this, you'll start to make natural assessments of who is or who isn't in alignment with you.

Have you ever been through a great life shift and afterwards found you just couldn't be around certain people? Perhaps they'd been your best friends but now they seem so out of sync with the person you are today? As we grow and learn while activating our life's purpose, our energy field changes vibration and with this our attraction or repulsion to others' energy shifts as well. When you sense a change in how you feel about someone to whom you were once close, try not to ignore it. Keep in mind that they may not have changed, but you have and that's what makes all the difference.

I can remember back in 2004 making a very conscious decision. I decided to step back from nearly every friend or acquaintance I had made in the self-development field. I also decided to step back from following anyone else's spiritual teachings. It was at this point in my career that soul told me *if I was ever to bring through my information, my way, then I had to stop surrounding myself in the influence of others.*

At the time, this felt like a natural progression for me and actually it wasn't a hard decision at all. The people around me didn't understand *why* I had pulled away – and quite frankly, I didn't feel the need to tell them.

For me, this was a liberating period in my life. I felt as if I had given myself permission to explore my full range of capabilities – and I was off and flying. To this day, I still don't follow any other spiritual teacher's work, though I'm always open to learning. I focus on my soul and its teachings, which I bring through. I've found this works beautifully when focusing on being original and staying independent.

It's therefore vital that you trust in and use your originality. Copying from or imitating others takes so much of your energy away and dulls the shine of soul. You're here to express your unique talents and experiences *your way*, so that we all get to benefit from the colour and bounty you have to offer.

When each of us is focused on our own originality we can stop the competitiveness and instead become inspired and propelled ahead by one another. As conscious Cosmic Messengers this can become our new reality and our new way. All it takes is your willingness and effort to evolve.

Forging your own path

If you're ready to embrace your originality and step back from anyone or any situation that is out of alignment with your core focus, you'll notice that your life path begins to accelerate. When you're unhindered by constraint or trying to fit in, you'll be free to create in your most unique way. You'll also find that you start to build up trust in yourself and your abilities, as you're not relying on anyone else to prop you up.

Now there are varying degrees to which we forge our own path. Some people have the urge to be leaders, not only of their own life but in those of others as well. These people may be driven in their approach to their career or chosen avenue of self-expression. Then there are people who feel more at ease not taking the lead but instead being in a support role to others – because that's where their unique skill sets shine.

Leadership shows itself through many different guises. As you decide to take a unique and personal approach to your life, you'll discover leadership skills that perhaps you never knew you had or which have lain dormant since childhood.

Rather than being sidetracked from your path, it's important that you stay on it and utilize your soul experiences. Why not start coming up with creative ways to achieve your goals, your way? And don't be too quick to look over your shoulder at what everyone else is doing.

When you start to forge your own path it can seem that you're the one out ahead and that others are behind you or not in sight. This is simply an illusion created by the personality, which often views your human life as a race from birth to death. Remind yourself that your life isn't a race and that the only person you have to contend with and please is yourself.

✳ PRACTICE ✳
Discover your unique skills

To help you rediscover and then focus on implementing your unique life skills, I offer you the following practice:

1. Test yourself. Nothing teaches us better how capable we are than self-application. Set yourself a small goal each day in which you're using *one* of the skills that you're good at. For example, if you're a natural conversationalist, create situations where you need to engage with others and practise communicating.

You could do this online in a blog, or via social media or email. Or you could start a group in person to help people open up with one another. Start to apply the ideas that you come up with, no matter how small.

2. Use your skills every day. I must stress the importance of creating a pattern: using your skills as one-offs or intermittently won't be enough to prove to your personality what you're consistently good at. To use your skills each day, set realistic goals that can be easily accomplished.

3. Give yourself credit. Once you're testing out your skills and using them on a daily basis, ensure that you remember to give yourself credit. Being rewarded is important to the personality, as it builds a sense of accomplishment. If you keep your personality happy, you're well on the way to expanding your life purpose.

The power of being on your own

When you start focusing on being the original soul that you came here to be, you'll discover that you're intrinsically drawn to spending more time on your own. This is one aspect of fulfilling your life purpose and becoming a Cosmic Messenger that can scare some people and often make them withdraw from the next level of life. On the other hand, some people just love receiving 'alone time', especially if they've spent most of their life giving to others and not put any energy into themselves.

When I was going through my long waking-up process from the mid- to late-90s, I too felt the call to be on my own. It was an innate need to withdraw from the familiar, so that I could be in deep contemplation with my soul. Have you ever felt this way and if so, have you followed through and created some space for self-reflection?

Being on your own can be one of the most liberating experiences of your life. Coming to rely upon and know our own capabilities is something that (sometimes) can only be done on our own. It is far from being a lonely experience, too: once you give over to spending time with yourself, soul's voice starts to become much clearer.

You'll find that you can hear your inner guidance without outside noises deafening the voice within. You'll also be able to establish a more secure connection to your guides and Angels in spirit. The stillness surrounding you creates an environment conducive to receiving and relaying messages from the spiritual dimension.

Now keep in mind that being on your own doesn't have to mean blocking out all connection with others. For some it could simply mean putting aside one or two nights a week to be quiet and away from noisy social interactions. For others it might happen on select weekends, and others still may choose to be on their own full-time or before or after work each day. Choose what feels right for you, but do know that the more time and space you can devote to stillness and quiet reflection, the more rapidly the expansion of your life purpose can take place.

CHAPTER 12

Living Your Next Level

W e're now coming to a chapter of *Cosmic Messengers* that will begin to set you up for the next level of your life.

Forming a higher vision

Have you ever considered that your human life (and soul life) evolves in levels? Just imagine a spiral. If you look down at a spiral from above it appears to be flat, with energy moving from the centre outwards or from outwards within. Look at images of our Milky Way spiral galaxy, as it depicts this beautifully.

Now imagine that you're viewing this spiral side on, seeing it from a three-dimensional viewpoint. Using our example of the Milky Way, you'll notice that the galactic core is the central point of the spiral, with our Sun and all other planetary bodies moving around it. Planetary bodies are in perpetual motion along the spiral of life. And given that we too are a planetary body, the same can be said of us.

Now imagine that the spiral is not only moving outwards and inwards but also up or down. We could say that there are *levels* within a spiral. We could say that moving through the levels of a spiral is the act of *evolution* itself. Have you ever considered this?

You (as a planetary body) are evolving in a spiral of consciousness. At the centre is soul (the galactic core) and your human life spirals through levels of experiences, sending information back and forth to your eternal 'beingness'. As you evolve, you're moving around the spiral of life.

In and out of centre

From human birth we begin to move out from centre, and just before our death we move back into our core. On a daily basis we're moving in and out of centre – depending on our experiences – all the while moving through the spiral of evolution. As we evolve, so too does the core of the cosmos, which is our home.

Our individual evolution promotes cosmic evolution. When consciously choosing to spiral upwards and evolve your life, it helps if you can rise above and see the bigger picture forming. This is where your imagination (along with focused meditation) comes into its own. Having a far-reaching vision for your life is pivotal in forming a destination to work towards. Your destination forms part of your life purpose.

✴ PRACTICE ✴
See the bigger picture

Back in Chapter 3, I spoke about ways to re-kindle your talents and skills from childhood, to assist you in remembering why you're here and what your life purpose is. As you start to consciously walk upon your life path, an essential practice is to regularly rise up (and tune in to) the bigger picture that your daily action steps are forming. To do this, I suggest the following exercise:

1. Whenever you find a free moment in your day, allow your mind to drift off and go soft. Focus on the goals that you're working towards and as you do this, ask soul: 'Show me the higher vision that is forming.'

2. Simply asking is enough to trigger images in your mind's eye (your third eye, at the centre of your brain). You may notice that you seemingly rise up above the planet and look down upon yourself living out your most precious desires.

3. Try not to judge the feelings, ideas or images that come to you. Simply observe and say 'thank you'. Then go about your day with this higher vision firmly in mind.

As you regularly rise above and tune in to your higher visions, you'll notice that your motivation increases. Having that vision to work towards can give you the inner confidence to continue forward on days when it's hard to stay on track.

That *higher* (long-range) vision creates your momentum, which then gives rise to resistance, as we discussed in Chapter 8. Remember, the more resistance you encounter, the greater heights you're soaring to.

Making firm decisions

Another soul-enriching development that occurs when taking your life to the next level of consciousness is an increasing ability to make productive and firm decisions. As you rise in awareness and start creating space (and stillness) before making any decisions, you'll be growing in maturity.

The more mature and wise you become, the more you'll accelerate your growth to the next level. As a Cosmic Messenger, it's your awareness that you're a contributing energy to universal growth that triggers soul to rise into its full potential. For when we know the far-reaching effects of our actions, we do pull in and consider before making important decisions.

I suggest that you start looking for opportunities to be firm in your choices. Hold it within your energy field that you're an attractor of making the right decision for yourself, in the moment. Experience will be your best teacher, so the more practice you can get, the better.

Extending past your comfort zone

Look for situations to arise that demand your full attention. Rather than drifting off and not being present when making a choice that may require you to extend past your comfort zone, instead face and embrace your ability to decide. This is your unique life path that you're forging, and it requires you to support and back yourself up by owning your decisions.

A good indicator of how well you're embracing conscious decision-making will be your feelings towards old situations that keeping popping back in for a rerun. Perhaps you've had trouble communicating with your family in the past, or perhaps other people's attitudes have rubbed you up the wrong way?

Being knowingly (or unknowingly) drawn into others' dramas can drain your energy and spiral you downwards from centre and away from your higher visions. We've all experienced this at some time in our life. What you'll find when you're spiralling up in consciousness is that the old situations no longer bother you as they once did. You'll also find that you don't attract them as often as you used to – and even if you do, you'll make empowered choices not to engage, but instead to grow your compassion and resilience all at once.

Consistency is key

Taking your life to the next level also requires a consistent diligence and effort on your part. By applying yourself in the direction of your desires each day, you'll be establishing a pattern of *personal excellence*.

How does the idea of personal excellence sound to you? Does it make you grow a little taller and more expansive or does it make you pull in with uncertainty? *Personal excellence is natural to soul*, yet it may be foreign to the personality. We grow our level of excellence through our applied actions each day. The more focused you are, particularly having your higher vision in mind, the easier it becomes to stay consistent.

UNIVERSAL SECRET 12:
'Be consistently aware.'

Just think about it. Right now you're already a natural at consistency. There are everyday patterns you've created and have no trouble at all repeating. Yes? Perhaps it's that morning coffee or your journey to work? Perhaps you go to the gym each night or regularly eat a certain food?

Consistency is what creates our experiences of tomorrow. Now if you consistently decide to create patterns and behaviours that support your life purpose, and if you can remain steady in their application, you'll serve to accelerate your life to the next level of being.

I credit consistency for enabling me to be where I am today, writing this book for you and continually taking myself to the next level of life. I made a decision back in 2000 to do what I needed to do in order to be working for myself in the holistic field, using my talents and skills to support and grow my lifestyle in the process. I had a 10-year plan in mind in which to achieve this.

My destination allowed me to chart my course. Once I got past the 10-year mark and had established a good pattern that proved my ideas worked, I kept going and growing. There were many things during the first decade that brought great challenge and tested my resolve. I could have given up at any stage, but I didn't because my higher vision kept calling to me and consistency kept me on track.

Having this vision made all the difference, as it reminded me of why I was doing what I was doing and how it was fulfilling my purpose in the process. You're going to be consistent anyway (humans tend to be creatures of habit), so why not be *consciously consistent*? As you make firm decisions that support your higher vision, life naturally evolves and spirals upwards, level by level. As someone who is focused on being an aware Cosmic Messenger, you have such power available to you.

In any moment you can turn your life around by reminding yourself that you're a pivotal part of the universal whole. You were born of cosmic origins, and it's your birthright to be a creator of love and beauty along your divine life path. The sooner you decide to take on the mantle of self-responsibility that comes with being a Cosmic Messenger, the sooner the magic, meaning and reward will flood into your life.

Staying flexible

Another essential in taking your life to the next level is your ability to be *flexible and open to change*, as and when it's needed. Now staying flexible doesn't imply that you'll change your mind on a whim and forgo firm decision-making. What is does mean is that your awareness allows you to be in the cosmic flow, rather than trying to control situations from the limited perspective of your personality alone.

In Chapter 6, I spoke about cosmic energy and how it influences our life on Earth. There are days when it's easier to achieve your goals and days when it's best to rest. As you learn to intuit, sense and work with cosmic energy, you'll find that being flexible becomes a by-product of being in the flow. The cosmos is always presenting us with opportunities that are perfect for manifesting our desires.

If you keep a rigid outlook on how your desires will unfold, and the timeline for this happening, you'll miss out on the incredible wealth of abundance being offered to you. On numerous occasions I've been rewarded for going with my gut instinct, listening to the signs and changing my course. It becomes a way of life, particularly the more I open up to it. Rather than getting frustrated when my plans change, I almost come to expect it now.

For when you work with the universe as a conscious Cosmic Messenger, you'll discover that your intuition rises and that you'll come to predict when and how energy is about to shift. This is what causes you to rise to a whole new level. You'll set your own benchmark and consistently enjoy meeting it and then raising it. One of the poetic side effects of becoming aware as a Cosmic Messenger is that your standards naturally progress and lift, in accordance with the higher visions you're tuning in to and acting upon.

Flexibility gives rise to spontaneity, which is a hugely beneficial life skill you can nurture as you take your life to that next level. The better able you are to decide in the moment and adjust your focus as required, the quicker rewards come to you. It's when we're stuck in our ways and refuse to change that we stagnate in consciousness and miss out on the golden opportunities to excel that the universe consistently offers us. Decide to embrace flexibility and your purpose will deepen and become more clearly known to you.

Realizing your dreams

Finally, as you consciously take your life to the next level, be prepared to realize your dreams. We've spoken at length throughout *Cosmic Messengers* about the importance of identifying our desires so we can imagine them and then act upon them, bringing them into form with the assistance of the universe.

Your dreams are the basis for your reality. As you apply the processes laid out in each chapter of this book, your life will begin to accelerate and your desires will start to come to fruition. Be ready for this, as your life purpose also develops and becomes known to you.

There truly is no greater joy than to feel yourself a part of the cosmic flow. To experience first-hand the manifestation of your desires, and to know that it was *you* working with the universe (as a team) that produced them, is as humbling as it's awe-inspiring. At each little victory along the course of your life path, remember to stop, pause, reflect and give thanks. It's this self-recognition that reminds you of who you are and what you're capable of here on Earth.

Setting yourself goals

I suggest that when you feel an upswing in energy and you've been doing the daily work of accelerating your life, you consciously take yourself to the next level. You can do this by deciding to drop old, limiting ways. Perhaps you've been considering giving up or cutting back on alcohol, smoking, drug taking, binge eating, junk food, swearing, or any other addictive habit that may interfere with your sensitivity.

Take one of these habits and decide that 'today's the day'. Decide to shift that habit and remember not to tell anyone, because the power of secrecy will ensure that you stick to your new healthy lifestyle choice.

Mark the date and your decision in your diary or planner, perhaps using code so only you know about it. Then start to live this next level straight away. Use any resistance you feel to propel yourself forward. Chances are, you'll be so quietly excited at your empowering choice that any resistance you encounter will serve to fuel you ahead.

As soon as you've accomplished one goal and met one desire, soul will be setting another for you. *Complacency has no place within the fabric of a Cosmic Messenger.*

It's the nature of soul to be in a constant flow of creativity, so look forward to being occupied and challenged as you realize your dreams. Just imagine what your life is like at that next level. You'll be fulfilling your legacy and reflecting the very essence of the universe – for just like nature you're in a constant state of evolution. You're an eternal energy beloved one, and you were born to realize your dreams.

CHAPTER 13

You Are a Cosmic Messenger

We now come to a most important aspect of living your life with purpose. If you've been reading and working with the chapters preceding this one and are now living as someone who embraces cosmic consciousness, then something quite remarkable begins to happen. You may be noticing this already.

World service

As you take personal responsibility for your path and are manifesting your desires in communion with the universe, it follows that you'll naturally be developing into someone who is involved with *world service*.

What does the idea of world service mean to you? Is it something that you find intriguing or does it repel you? Do you consider that world service will ask a lot of you or that it's reserved for those who came here to publicly lead others? What if I told you that world service is natural to soul? World service is something that each of us encapsulates as we become aware Cosmic Messengers.

UNIVERSAL SECRET 13:
'Soul naturally loves to give of itself and be in service.'

You may have grown up thinking that the last thing you want to do is be in service to the world around you. After all, where does that leave you? Will you be drained and lost, simply existing to serve others? Will serving the world limit your ability to manifest your own desires? Well, I invite you to consider something quite different indeed.

Once you're realizing your purpose and utilizing your natural talents and skills, you'll accordingly be considering how you can help the world around you. This is a consequence of opening up to the cosmos and the bounty it provides. For the cosmos is always giving its goodness unhindered and you're a part of this cosmic flow.

It's natural for you to give of yourself. If anything, we tend to hold back our goodness before we've woken up and have started to carve out a conscious life path. It's after we've opened our heart and soul is leading the way that we realize by giving of who we are, we actually realize the power of the universe through us. Rather than draining ourselves, we fill ourselves up with greater energy. The more we give of who we are, the more we receive back that goodness.

Giving of yourself

Now *giving of yourself* becomes self-replenishing when you're on purpose. It's almost as if you can't help but ask, 'How can I best serve?' You'll continually come up with ways to implement your skills that will benefit not only yourself but others as well.

For example, when I first woke up and began working towards a holistic career, I found myself inexplicably drawn to sharing what I was discovering each day. I'd tell anyone who cared to listen what I was learning about spirit and soul and the amazing opportunity we have to create the life path of our dreams. As I did this and could hear myself back, it actually reinforced what I was sharing and made it become more tangible and real for me.

I was being personally topped up as I delivered my message to others. That spirit of desiring to share my knowledge and experience is as strong today (perhaps stronger) than it ever was. I get so excited writing my weekly energy forecasts and daily posts on social media, as I share my passion and knowledge with the world around me.

The only potential trap in world service is giving yourself over to what you think you know before you've actually done the work yourself. This is an easy trap to fall into, because once you open up to the cosmos and world of spirit, the personality naturally wants to share everything, even before you've had a chance to test out your newfound theories on life. Has this ever happened to you? Perhaps it's happening now?

The way around this pitfall is to ensure you use discernment when sharing your information, talents and skills. Use your growing awareness: when you hear yourself extolling spiritual virtues to others, make sure you're applying them in your own life as well. In other words, *walk your talk.*

World service is a joyous by-product of being a Cosmic Messenger. One could even say that when we step into *universal service* we open our heart and let our true nature flow, unhindered. I suggest you look for ways that you can be of service right now. Rather than holding back, give more of yourself. Do this for yourself, please yourself first and foremost, and know that by doing so, you'll be helping others and the wider cosmic community in the process.

Your role as a Cosmic Messenger

Now we come to the very essence of this book, for you are a *Cosmic Messenger.* As you awaken to who you are and consciously become aware of the world and universal forces of which you're a part, you step into a new era of personal excellence. Extending your energy to meet the cosmos reminds you of your role as a Cosmic Messenger.

Cosmic Messengers are messengers of the cosmos. In our everyday life we're constantly passing on and receiving messages from one another. Think about it – that's all we tend to do. We're natural communicators. The rise of social media is proof of this. Imagine that the messages you share and transmit can be done so with cosmic awareness in mind.

Every time you think and have the opportunity to speak or act, you do so with your bigger picture to the fore. Are you doing this now? Or is this something you can work on achieving each day?

I invite you to embrace yourself as a Cosmic Messenger. No matter what your purpose, your career or your lifestyle, you're able to tune in to cosmic energy and be personally responsible for every creative act of your day. Can you imagine how the world would evolve if *everyone* took on the mantle of their cosmic responsibility?

Of course, this doesn't happen all at once, for we're all at different levels of evolution. However, if we can *increase the tipping point* between those who've woken up and those who haven't, we can improve the level of peace and personal satisfaction here on Earth.

Cosmic Messengers…

Hold their higher vision in mind, always.

Think before they speak.

Create space around their words, decisions and actions.

*Act with discernment and grow themselves by
learning and maturing through their experiences.*

*Aren't afraid of making mistakes and
being their genuine selves.*

Give themselves permission to be self-expressive and creative.

Accept challenges and look for opportunities to excel.

Push past their comfort zone.

*Show compassion and respect for all life forms and
consider the wider cosmic community their family.*

*Open their heart to the spiritual dimension
and do their best to lead with soul.*

*Focus on being an original, as they bring
through their natural talents and skills.*

Show reverence for all, and mostly for themselves.

You are a Cosmic Messenger.

*You have the universe at your call. How
will you choose to proceed?*

Loving your life purpose

Whether you have an exacting idea of your purpose or a more holistic one, what does develop as you embrace your cosmic consciousness and become a Cosmic Messenger is a love of humanity and your life path.

On countless occasions I've heard people say that they don't like other humans and would rather not be here. Have you ever heard something similar? When I hear this it spurs me on to focus even more deeply on being a Cosmic Messenger. How can we not love souls who choose the human vehicle to learn and express through? It's no different than the form of animals, plants and minerals. It's so important that we connect and love the souls that choose physical forms to express through.

As you begin to activate your purpose – as you live with purpose each day – you'll find that love does swell within your heart. Your heart's energy centre cracks open, almost like an egg, and spills out the soul that is your core, your essence – and that is you, *Cosmic Messenger*. To be on purpose, it's vital to start loving what you do and what you are right now. Even if you're unsure of your next steps, be in love with the moment.

You came here to this lifetime encompassing a sum total of experiences previously learned on Earth or elsewhere. You had an idea in the universal (and your individual) mind of what it was you wished to express and what your purpose for being would be. Each step along the way has served as an opportunity to remember the life you led before you entered a human body, so that you can realize the cosmos within you.

Just accepting your cosmic reality gives rise to loving your purpose. How can we not be in awe of the journey that we've led and continue to lead for eternity? It's magical, inspiring and sobering all at once. So ask yourself each day, Cosmic Messenger, 'Am I loving what I'm involved with?'

If your answer is 'yes', then continue on in the same vein. If your answer is 'no', then stop and take note. Ask yourself, 'How can I shift my focus to love?' Listen to the voice of soul quietly rising within you and then take note of what you're hearing by choosing to act on it. There's no greater channel in the universe than the voice of your soul. Trust in your own advice and run with it.

Being on purpose happens naturally when we're being creative and focused on bringing through beauty. Beauty is an energy that's flowing and connects with the cosmos. You already are that beauty at your core. You're beauty by nature. Embrace who you are, Cosmic Messenger, and set about realizing the full potential of the universe by using your life as an example.

Satisfaction, fulfilment and reward

As you move forward, living on purpose and stopping regularly to be thankful and in gratitude for your life's path, you'll automatically generate a sense of personal satisfaction, fulfilment and reward. I can remember in my mid-20s feeling unsatisfied; I was searching for deeper meaning in my life and that search felt all-consuming. Perhaps you've felt the same way?

I couldn't believe that I was just here to be born, go to school, grow up, find a career, meet someone, keep on working and then one day, die. Even as I write this now, I can't quite comprehend that mindset. I always knew there was more to life than meets the eye, and I'm so glad that soul kicked me into gear to find out what lies beneath the surface of our physical reality.

As Cosmic Messengers actively engaged in world service by living our life on purpose, there will be countless moments in each day when we'll be filled up with an immense sense of awe. To appreciate this and receive your rewards, it's crucial to slow down often and just reflect.

I do this several times every day. I literally put down what I'm doing, look up at the sky or walk outside into nature and just comprehend the personal effort that brought me to where I am right now. I do my best to marvel at my path with a childlike awe. When you do this, you immediately receive back the goodness you put out. And this is what fills you up with the deepest satisfaction possible.

Knowing that your life matters and that you're making a difference in the universe because of who you are, using your talents and skills, is priceless. It builds value and worth and enables you to continue on, refreshed and invigorated for another day.

Cosmic Messenger, embrace your role this lifetime. Accept the praise and compliments that will come to you. Allow others to receive the gift of expressing their truth to you, by not shying away from the acknowledgement you'll receive. And freely give your own admiration of others. In this divided physical dimension, we can't have giving without receiving: together they form one cohesive whole. You're here to be a symbol of beauty. Work your magic well.

The Cosmic Reasons for Physical, Emotional, Mental and Spiritual Issues

This guide will help you to understand how we can be affected and influenced by cosmic events. Throughout *Cosmic Messengers* I've spoken about energy and raising our awareness to accelerate our life purpose. When you're constantly doing this, you'll find that you're naturally upgraded on a physical, emotional, mental and spiritual level.

As these upgrades occur, you'll find it very helpful to check in with this guide, as it provides you with direction and solace for what you're going through. Refer to this guide regularly and come to know how the cosmic shifts affect your life

To be aware of when cosmic energy shifts are occurring, I suggest you follow my Tip-Off Global Energy Forecast, which can be found at https://www.elizabethperu.com

Note: The information given below should not be treated as a substitute for professional medical advice; always consult a medical practitioner.

The Sun and its cycles

As Cosmic Messengers, one of the most potent cosmic events that can influence us is the flaring of the Sun. Imagine that the Sun, which is our life-giving star, powers our energy body. We're intrinsically linked to the Sun and its cycles.

The ancients knew this and honoured the Sun for the powerful influence it wields over human life. Countless civilizations, dating back tens of thousands of years, expressed their reverence for the Sun and its sustaining and nourishing properties, through architecture, poetry, song, dance, art, the sciences and healing therapies.

The Sun can also be responsible for the disruption of our electrical fields, and irradiation on Earth. We need to approach the Sun, like all planetary bodies, with a sense of inner connection and deep respect. We can think of the Sun as *the soul* of our solar system. Its energy connects directly with our heart, solar plexus and third eye (pineal gland).

The Sun produces pure white light and is the source of white light in the physical dimension. When we're absorbing solar rays, we're flooding our body in white light, which contains the full spectrum of healing energy.

Sunrise and sunset

The most advantageous time to be soaking in the Sun's rays is at sunrise or sunset. Simply raise your arm to shoulder height and if the Sun falls below this, you're being bathed in a therapeutic level of light.

At sunrise and sunset the Sun's rays are like a healing vitamin pill for our energy body, as our skin, eyes and energy field absorb the long-range healing waves of orange and red.

At other times of the day, the Sun's rays can be particularly harsh (when the shorter wavelengths of green and blue are absorbed) – this allows solar radiation to enter Earth's field and penetrate our energy body.

Solar flares, CMEs, geomagnetic activity and energy sensitivity

Solar flares occur when there are massive eruptions on the Sun's surface. Coronal mass ejections, or CMEs, often follow solar flares. It's the CMEs that hurl out solar radiation into space, via the ensuing solar wind (plasma ejection).

When CMEs are Earth-facing, they may take between one and four days to reach our outer atmosphere. The shockwave from CMEs can interact with Earth's magnetosphere, causing a geomagnetic storm and auroras at Earth's magnetic poles. This can result in radio signal interruptions, GPS malfunctions and disturbances in power grids, pipelines and satellite transmissions.

Now, despite this potential disturbance to Earth's field, science still claims that humans are not physically affected by solar activity. However, I've found quite the opposite to be true. Whenever the Sun is busy producing solar flares that may or may not produce CMEs, those *sensitive to energy* are particularly affected.

If you're sensitive to energy you pick up on energy shifts easily. Your energy field is quite large and in tune with the spiritual as well as the physical dimension. More and more people are becoming sensitive to energy, as they open up to their cosmic consciousness and start living a clean and healthy lifestyle. Sensitive people pick up on solar activity *as* it's happening on the Sun, regardless of whether solar flares ever produce CMEs that are Earth-directed.

Solar minimum and maximum

Every 11 years or so, the Sun moves through a different cycle of activity that's often referred to as *solar minimum* and *solar maximum*.

Solar minimum is the cycle of least activity of the Sun and solar maximum is the cycle of most activity. During solar maximum we tend to see lots of flares on the Sun that are labelled M and X class (X class are the largest flares, while M class are 10 times less powerful than X). Solar minimum is also interesting in that more cosmic radiation infiltrates Earth's field during this period. Both periods in the Sun's cycle provide us with an incredible opportunity to rise in consciousness.

The Sun shifts our consciousness

The Sun's activity directly impacts our deeper conscious awareness. As the Sun goes through a growth cycle, so do we. There are portals of energy that link the Sun and Earth, and everyone's energy field – regardless of how sensitive they are to energy – has access to the upshifts that the Sun's activity provides us with.

Symptoms associated with solar activity

Below are the physical, emotional and mental symptoms that can occur during periods of heightened solar activity. I find that energetically aware and sensitive people tend to get these symptoms whenever the Sun is active, and regardless of whether solar flares produce CMEs that are Earth-directed.

Physical symptoms

- Whenever the Sun is active you may get random tension headaches that occur mostly over the eyes, as your third eye is being activated. Migraines can also be triggered.

- Sleep is interrupted. You may wake up at double digital times: 2:22, 3:33, 4:44 a.m., etc. The energy of this master number timing connects you with the cosmic flow. (*See also Chapter 9*).

- You could feel lethargic and lacking in energy. Your body is being energetically rewired during solar activity.

- You may feel an inner heat rise within you.

- You may also feel dizzy and ungrounded. Physical exercise is a fantastic balancer during solar activity.

- Your ears may be receiving high-vibration downloads. This sounds like a tuning fork being struck in one ear or the other. (See the section on *ear downloads* in Reference Guide 1 for more information.)

- Your neck and shoulders could become tense and stiff. Stretch your body regularly to assist with movement, as this expels electrical charge out of your system.

- During periods of strong solar activity, drink more fresh, filtered water, as dehydration is common.

- During geomagnetic storms in particular, you could also feel extra hungry. Our physical body uses more energy, and therefore requires greater fuel, during the days after a solar flare, CME and subsequent solar storm around Earth.

- Increasing physical exercise helps counteract any short-term weight gain and it also counterbalances any excessive electrical charge moving though our bodies during geomagnetic storms.

Emotional symptoms
- You could become teary, and feel a sense of loss. This is because you're releasing old habits and toxins from your cells and are upshifting in consciousness.

Mental symptoms
- You could become easily bored with your daily routine. Solar activity pushes us to be more creative.

- You may also find that you're flooded with insight and inspiration. Have a notebook handy to take down your musings.

- Your mind may be racing. Perhaps you find it hard to focus? This energy will pass. Ride it out.

Spiritual symptoms
- Soul pushes through to be heard during solar activity, so you could be questioning your current path and direction. Clarity will come from this.

Solar and lunar eclipses

Twice every year (and more rarely, three times) we experience the cosmic event of the eclipses. A solar eclipse occurs when the Moon passes between the Sun and Earth, either partially or fully blocking the light of the Sun. A lunar eclipse occurs when Earth moves in between the Sun and the Moon, as the Moon passes either fully or partially through Earth's shadow.

Perhaps more so than any other cosmic event, the eclipses deliver a sense of awe and a deeper connection with the cosmos of which we're a part. We quite literally *can't ignore* the eclipses when they happen, for they shake life up on nearly every level and give us a regularly spaced *cosmic clean-out*.

There's a *distinct season* that occurs during the eclipse cycle. It consists of two-weeks-apart periods that give us paced space in which to integrate the changes that the eclipse season brings.

The pre-eclipse period

This period begins two weeks prior to the first actual eclipse of the season. During this period we're planning for incoming newness and upgrades to our lifestyle. At the same time we're clearing out what no longer serves us; we're releasing old patterns and putting empowered boundaries in place.

The in-between eclipse period (the eclipse doorway)

An energetic doorway opens up just after the first eclipse of the season takes place. This *eclipse doorway* signals the start of a period where every focused thought and feeling that we have is intensified, bringing through near-instant manifestation.

The eclipse doorway is one of advanced opportunity as we experience a rise in cosmic consciousness. During this period it's vital that you let go every day and allow the universe to guide you. You're in 'observer mode' as you gather images and ideas that you'll implement once the eclipse season completes.

Signs will be everywhere and soul will be leading. A doorway on a new, upgraded lifestyle opens for you, as over the period until the next eclipse of the season, you're creating a new, empowered way of living.

The post-eclipse period

At the final eclipse of the season, the eclipse doorway closes and we begin the post-eclipse period. This two-week period closes down the season that began back at the opening of the pre-eclipse period.

During the post-eclipse we're moving ahead. We're embedding the new and upgraded lifestyle we've been working on all eclipse season. This is when we *take action*, making any last changes to those intentions we initiated at the opening of the season.

The eclipse family

Eclipses occur in series, or what I call *families*. The series of eclipses is also known as *the Saros cycle*. The stargazers of antiquity mapped eclipse seasons with great precision, observing a cycle of approximately 18 years between a recurrence of the exact alignment of the Sun, Moon and Earth.

Every eclipse season triggers a specific alignment of Earth to both the Sun and the Moon. Therefore, every eclipse season brings forward slightly different lessons, gifts and challenges, depending on how exactly the planetary alignments are arranged and which energies they trigger within us.

The first eclipse of the cycle is when the family is born. Then, approximately every 18 years, there's another exact eclipse (Sun, Moon and Earth alignment) as the family grows and matures. The family eventually closes down with the last eclipse of the cycle. Eclipse family life cycles can span many hundreds of years.

The solar eclipse

The solar eclipse is always accompanied by a new moon. New moons signal freshness and a reset; they supercharge the eclipse with the energy *of new beginnings.*

Solar eclipses bring us heightened inspiration and accelerated energy and can also bring on *ascension symptoms.* Ascension refers to the evolution of your soul by the raising of consciousness. In other words, the more aware you become of your place within the universe as a Cosmic Messenger, the faster you evolve in your human life. Ascension doesn't mean leaving the planet and your physical body.

Solar eclipses accelerate our awareness of who we are naturally, and they activate our masculine and action-based energy. If you can meditate when a solar eclipse is happening, you can tap into a stream of high-vibration cosmic energy that directly activates your heart and brain. This then aligns personality and soul (head and heart) and makes it easier for you to comprehend your human life and move onto your life purpose as a knowing (soulful) human being.

Symptoms associated with the solar eclipse

The following symptoms are commonly experienced throughout the entire eclipse season, which is one of the most intense cosmic periods of each year.

Physical symptoms

- If you've been preparing and doing your daily life work in the pre-eclipse period and have been shedding old habits, you'll likely feel enlivened and physically reset by a solar eclipse. You may be full of energy on the day of the eclipse, with a sense of inner excitement at your imminent rebirth.

- Ideas and inspiration can be flowing, as sleep patterns are disrupted significantly.

- If you've been resisting change in the pre-eclipse period you may experience the following physical disruptions: headaches, nausea, sore eyes, a blocked or runny nose, sore muscles, blocked ears, lack of energy and low motivation.

  These symptoms arise because your body wants to shed as part of its natural process, and yet you've mentally been resisting (perhaps fearing) these shifts. It's best if you can allow your body to lead you. Follow the messages you receive.

- Massage and any form of bodywork are brilliant for helping you easily to eliminate toxicity from your cells and release stuck energy.

Emotional symptoms

- Our close relationships are often affected by a solar eclipse, so if there's any area in which you've been out of balance with a partner, family member or friend, it could come to an abrupt head at this time.

You can soften the blow of any relationship shifts brought on by the solar eclipse by doing your work in the pre-eclipse period. This means in the two weeks before an eclipse, try not to overlook what your intuition is telling you. Speak up, as and when you need to. Listen to your gut instinct. Make small changes daily.

- You could be teary on the day of a solar eclipse. Crying is a natural form of physical release, so allow the water to flow. You'll feel better for it.

- Passions could be high, so be responsible for yourself and keep in mind that not everyone may be on the same wavelength as you during a solar eclipse.

Mental symptoms

- Solar eclipses can increase the rate at which our brainwaves vibrate. Your beta (active) brainwave state could accelerate, meaning you'll be flooded with thoughts, ideas and inspiration. Be ready for this by having a notebook handy and writing down what comes to you.

- Some people can become heated, angry and frustrated, particularly if they're not used to being downloaded with creative thoughts.

- Steer clear of arguments and conflict on the day of a solar eclipse, as you could do and/or say what you may later regret.

Spiritual symptoms

- Spiritually, we have a grand opportunity to spiral up in cosmic consciousness during a solar eclipse. It's beneficial if you can meditate on the day, to tune in to the rise in cosmic awareness.

The lunar eclipse

The lunar eclipse is always accompanied by a full moon. Full moons bring with them release and completion, as they magnify the power of the eclipse and imbue us with the strength to let go.

Lunar eclipses bring us natural resolutions. During a lunar eclipse, emotions are more strongly felt than during a solar eclipse. The feminine energy within us is activated, making this period best suited to deep contemplation, healing and letting go.

Symptoms associated with the lunar eclipse

Physical symptoms

- Lunar eclipses can bring with them muscle stiffness and soreness. If you're resisting letting go of old patterns and physical pain, you could go through a bout of *spiritual flu* (*see Reference Guide 1*).

- Listen to your body during a lunar eclipse and try not to push yourself too hard.

- Your third eye may be clearing, increasing your spiritual visions (*see Reference Guide 1*). Headaches and runny noses are common, as your sinuses clear.

- This is a period for completion. You can help yourself by using water as therapy. Take a long walk outdoors if possible, to ground yourself.

- Cleanse by bathing with Epsom or Dead Sea salts, to help your body naturally detox and release.

Emotional symptoms

- More so than during a solar eclipse, emotions run very deep at this time. Women in particular may feel that every emotion is close to the surface of their skin, as they open up and allow their true feelings to be released.

- If you feel vulnerable, go out under the lunar eclipse energy and turn your palms up to the Moon. Feel your hands drawing in the eclipse energy to help balance and stabilize your energy field.

- This is an excellent period for a meaningful conversation with someone close. It's also an ideal time to journal your feelings.

Mental symptoms

- You could be feeling drained and fuzzy-headed. It's best not to plan any detailed activities that require mental aptitude during a lunar eclipse. Instead, focus on meditative and contemplative activities during this period.

- Your words may not be expressed clearly. Your mental expression is creative and non-linear during a lunar eclipse. This is a period for deeper personal expression with your words. Let your imagination guide you.

Spiritual symptoms

- A lunar eclipse can bring on great spiritual progression. The magnetic pull of the full moon, coupled with the eclipse energy, promises that we receive a double dose of release.

- Old patterns can now naturally leave. If there's any habit you wish to drop, do so under a lunar eclipse.

- Ask soul to show you the next steps for your life. Simply allow the lunar energy to reset your direction from the inside out.

- Plan on being involved with slower-paced activities during this period, as you try not to overtax yourself. You're healing and evolving as you let go.

The Moon and its cycles

Perhaps more so than any other planetary body, the Moon connects us personally with the cosmos. It provides us with a stunning visual of the spheres that we are, floating in space. Have you ever looked up at the Moon and wondered what it would feel like to be walking upon its surface, looking back on Earth? Does the Moon fascinate you, soothe you, and remind you of your cosmic connection?

Each of us on Earth is intrinsically linked to the cycles of the Moon. Every 29 days, the Moon moves through eight distinct cycles (or phases) as viewed from Earth. These are determined by the ever-changing angles of the Sun, Moon and Earth, as the Moon orbits Earth. The 29-day cycle is known as the lunar month.

We'll look at four distinct Moon cycles: the new moon, the first quarter moon, the full moon and the last or third quarter moon. However, there are *another four cycles* that complete the eightfold path of the Moon. These are as follows:

1. *Waxing crescent* is when the Moon is past new; sunlight increases upon the Moon's face and it's less than half full.

2. *Waxing gibbous* is when the Moon is more than half full and sunlight is still increasing on its face.

3. *Waning gibbous* follows after the full moon, when sunlight is decreasing on the Moon's face.

4. *Waning crescent* occurs after the third quarter moon, when sunlight increasingly diminishes until the new moon.

New moon

We begin our Moon cycle with a new moon. This occurs when the Moon is positioned between Earth and the Sun – during a 1–3 day period that's also known as the dark moon.

- At the new Moon, the Sun and the Moon conjoin (energetically join hands) and the Sun's light is not reflected on the face of the Moon from our perspective here on Earth.

- During the new moon we can't see the illuminated half of the Moon, which is why it appears to be dark.

- At the new moon we turn inwards to the light of soul. This is a period to be reflective, to go on an inner journey, and to consider what you desire to create in your life over the next six months.

- The new moon is a time for *new beginnings*. This is when we plant our ideas and write down our inspired visions, sending our intentions off into the universe for fruition over the coming month.

- At new moon, the energy is still and quiet. This is a time for focusing on your heart's desires and speaking with soul. The new moon connects us with hope and inspiration as we envision our future reality.

- Use the new moon period to meditate on your desires.

First quarter moon

This is a half-moon cycle, as we're seven days on from the new moon with seven days to go until the full moon; we're building up the lunar month. At the first quarter moon, the Moon is at a 90-degree angle to Earth and we only see half of it illuminated by the Sun's light.

- The first quarter moon is a time for checking in on the plans we seeded at the new moon. The energy is building up to reach a conclusion at next week's full moon.

- This is the period to fine-tune your plans and desires.

Full moon

When the Moon is full, the Moon, the Sun and Earth are all in near alignment as the sunlit face of the Moon faces Earth.

- The full moon is a time for releasing, letting go, celebration and completion. The cosmic energy is usually intense, as we feel an inner excitement bubbling over.

- This is the period of the month to see your projects come to fruition. The Moon's energy naturally draws out any imbalances within your physical, emotional, mental and spiritual bodies.

- We may be detoxing on many levels. Some people will enjoy this cycle of the Moon, and feel on a high, while others may be more attuned with the new moon cycle.

Third quarter moon

This is a half-moon cycle in which we're seven days on from the full moon with seven days to go until the new moon. At the third quarter moon, the Moon is at a 90-degree angle to Earth and we only see half of it illuminated by the Sun's light. We're closing down the lunar month.

- The third quarter moon is a time for reflection; we're quieter and more introspective now. It's a phase to be in gratitude for the month that has been, and it's usually not a time to begin anything anew.

Moon at apogee

The apogee point is when the Moon is furthest from Earth during its monthly orbit. This results in a slightly smaller-looking Moon from our perspective here on Earth.

- When the Moon is furthest from Earth we can be feeling a little *out on our own* and almost disconnected from our cosmic community. Some people may enjoy this energy and actually feel *freer* than at other times of the month.

- Take things at a slow and steady pace. Ground your projects into reality by taking one step at a time.

Moon at perigee

The perigee point is when the Moon is closest to Earth during its monthly orbit. This results in a larger-looking Moon from our perspective here on Earth.

- When the Moon is closest to Earth, we can expect all energy to be heightened – which can increase tension in our body – and emotions to run high.

- We're also more tuned in to the invisible dimension at this time of the month, making it easier to hear our soul's intuition and to communicate with spirit.

Supermoon

A supermoon occurs when the Moon is either new or full, and at its closest to Earth (perigee) at the same time. So we can have either a super new moon or a super full moon.

- Our consciousness accelerates during a supermoon, so we can expect to see increased master number sequences. These double and triple digits are signs that we're in the supermoon flow.

- During a super new moon all new beginnings are amplified and multiplied. The energy can seem intense, as we're cosmically pushed out of complacency and asked to make a stand for our life.

- Radical change can be implemented at the super new moon. This is a rare Moon cycle to take advantage of. Any projects begun under a super new moon will be super-charged for their entire lifetime.

- During a super full moon conclusions and letting go of the past are amplified. This energy is extremely intense, and many people feel an overwhelming rush to wrap up the past and wipe the slate clean.

- Sleep is often interrupted and difficult during a super full moon, as soul is extremely awake and pushing us to align with our highest interests. Lucid dreaming and out-of-body travel are also heightened.

Equinox

Twice each year, Earth's plane crosses over the centre of the Sun, as day and night are of near equal length. We call this period of time the equinox and it signals the changing of our seasons.

Spring equinox occurs around 19–21 March each year for the northern hemisphere and around 21–24 September for the southern hemisphere.

Autumn equinox occurs around 19–21 March each year for the southern hemisphere and around 21–24 September for the northern hemisphere.

- During the equinox we're asked to become still, as our energy is pulled within to the light of the soul. It's important to pause, give thanks for our life journey and meditate on our purpose during the equinox.

- In order to rise we need first to compress our energy, and this is what happens during the equinox. This energy period is perfect for changing your daily routine and bringing in new activities that see you leading a full, varied and content lifestyle. We're upshifted in cosmic consciousness at the equinox.

- Being outdoors is advisable, as nature will harmoniously bring your energy and physical body into balance on this sacred cosmic occasion.

Solstice

Once a year the Sun will reach its lowest point at noon, which signals the winter solstice; and once a year the Sun will reach its highest point at noon, which signals the summer solstice.

Winter solstice occurs around 20–22 June for the southern hemisphere and around 20–22 December for the northern hemisphere.

Summer solstice occurs around 20–22 June for the northern hemisphere and around 20–22 December for the southern hemisphere.

Solstice marks the beginning of either summer or winter. Summer solstice marks the longest day of the year, as the most light is experienced. Every day after summer solstice the light decreases until it reaches a yearly low at winter solstice.

- Summer solstice brings us a culminating energy. The energy of the Sun is at its strongest and we're enjoying the rewards from the projects we began back at winter solstice. During this period we're celebrating and expanding our energy. We spend more time outdoors, giving thanks for the work we seeded in winter.

- Winter solstice marks the shortest day of the year, as the least light is experienced. Every day after winter solstice the light increases until it reaches a yearly high at summer solstice.

- Winter solstice brings us a reflective energy. The energy of the Sun is at its weakest and we're going within. It's during winter that we plan and work on the projects that will be fulfilled in summer. During this period we're quieter and in the design phase of our life. We work with the darker season to plant our creative seeds and nurture them slowly.

Planetary retrogrades

Due to Earth's tilt and its movement around the Sun, we regularly experience an apparent change in motion in the planetary bodies relative to Earth. Our planet is like a big spinning top, tilting on its axis by approximately 23 degrees. This tilt gives us the seasons across the globe.

When we say that a planet is in retrograde, it's meant purely from our perspective here on Earth – we have an Earth-centric view of the cosmos. So let's be clear, a retrograde doesn't mean that another planetary body is travelling backwards around the Sun in our solar system. It only appears to be doing so (visually) from here on Earth.

The planetary retrograde action is similar to driving along a motorway and overtaking the car next to you. As you prepare to overtake and drive alongside this car, it appears to stop as you become level with it. Then the car appears to move behind you, as you move ahead and overtake it. This optical illusion is what actually happens during a planetary retrograde. Earth appears to take over from the planetary body in its revolution around the Sun.

When a planetary body is in retrograde it generates an energy that sees us reversing over old ground. We're triggered to take a retrospective look and to glance back over our past. It's like shining a spotlight into the life we've led thus far.

You get to see what you may have missed and previously overlooked. You get to press the rewind button on experiences and events that you've lived through, but from an observer's perspective this time. In other words, you get a second chance to correct and shift the past.

I personally *love all planetary retrogrades* and encourage you to do the same. These periods of the year help us to fine-tune and hone our talents and skills, as we're slowed down and are cosmically encouraged to look at the closer details of our life. This energy is what makes us more resilient and able to upgrade our abilities. Let's now look at each of the planetary retrogrades in turn and what that means for you.

Chiron retrograde

Chiron is a large asteroid in our solar system that has significant pulls on our energy system. Chiron tends to influence us on the level of nostalgia and childhood wounds and experiences. Every year it moves in retrograde motion relative to Earth for approximately five months.

When Chiron is retrograde we start to relive old patterns and pain from our younger years – hurts that we felt we'd dealt with can come up for review. We're drawn back to what limits us, so that we can be released and set free via our acknowledgement of the past.

During Chiron retrograde you can:

- Take positive action to acknowledge the past patterns that keep you stuck.

- Heal any wounds in relation to how worthy you are, by taking positive actions today.

- Be responsible for clearing your past. Watch how you mature and grow *spiritually* during this period.

Jupiter retrograde

Jupiter is the largest known planet in our solar system – a giant whose size completely dwarfs that of Earth – with nearly 70 identified moons. As you can therefore imagine, Jupiter is a major planetary influencer in our lives.

Jupiter reminds us to expand and live large, without restricting our innate manifesting abilities. Every year it moves in retrograde motion relative to Earth for approximately four months. When Jupiter is retrograde it's the ideal time of the year to refine your relationship with abundance, as you:

- Plan new career moves and/or make changes to existing careers.

- Work on your relationship with abundance. Use your talents and skills to carve out your own niche.

- Allow yourself to receive, and to put strong boundaries in place.

- Expand beyond your limits and move way past your comfort zone.

Mars retrograde

Mars is a planet in our solar system that's only slightly smaller than Mercury – and I feel it was once very Earth-like. Mars has a robust planetary energy and reminds us that we need to take action in order to forge ahead with our destiny.

Mars moves retrograde only once every 2.2 years for a period of up to eight weeks, making its energies *acutely felt* when it does so.

- When Mars is retrograde we need to slow down and take a more considered approach to how we action the tasks of our everyday life. We begin to reassess our direction and carefully plan out our next steps.

- The Mars retrograde period is an ideal time to research and begin a new fitness and/or nutritional plan. We're also encouraged to reassess our boundaries within relationships and learn to be more self-expressive and personally empowered.

Mercury retrograde

Mercury is the planet that sits closest to the Sun in our solar system. Mercury is the messenger planet and it impacts everything on Earth that is electric, fast-moving and communicative, including our voice.

It also triggers our cheeky and playful side, so you can expect to be revved up and encouraged to have a strong sense of humour when Mercury takes a backwards glance through your life.

Each year Mercury moves in retrograde motion relative to Earth approximately every three months and for three weeks at a time. It's the planetary retrograde motion we get to work with the most often.

When Mercury is retrograde we become powerful agents of change, as:

- We revisit old relationships and get an opportunity to close off lingering energy and clear up past misunderstandings.

- We learn to become flexible, as plans can and will change at a moment's notice.

- We overhaul our personal communication style, as conversations reveal our hidden motivations.

- During Mercury retrograde, you become a *Cosmic Detective*, as you have a much stronger connection with your intuition and the spirit realm and can easily pick up on what other people are thinking.

Neptune retrograde

Neptune is the furthest known planet in our solar system, and being so far away from Earth, it affects us on a deep inner level. Neptune connects us with the invisible, spiritual dimension and works its magic through our dream states. Every year it moves in retrograde motion relative to Earth for approximately five months.

- When Neptune is retrograde it's the primary period of the year in which to explore soul's path and your life purpose.

This is when we delve into spiritual courses, books and the esoteric side of life.

During Neptune retrograde, our dream messages become vivid. Many people start to explore and experience lucid dreaming, and out-of-body experiences raise our cosmic consciousness.

Pluto retrograde

Pluto is located beyond Neptune. I still consider Pluto to be a planet (it was reclassified as a dwarf planet in 2006), and know that it has a direct pull on our deep (darker) and often hidden aspects.

Pluto influences us to accept all aspects of who we are, by shining a light into our past. Every year it moves in retrograde motion relative to Earth for approximately five months.

- When Pluto is retrograde we naturally begin to go over old ground and look into the matter of our personal power. Old hurts and pains naturally release from our body and we could get down on ourselves. You can counteract this by being all of who you are, rather than hiding what you love for fear of being judged or not accepted.

- Pluto retrograde is your yearly opportunity to forgive, release and heal your past – this can include past lives.

Saturn retrograde

Saturn is the second largest known planet in our solar system. Its mammoth size makes it a planetary heavyweight and it wields a huge influence on our lives. Saturn reminds us that our purpose matters and that we must take responsibility for the way that our life evolves. Every year it moves in retrograde motion relative to Earth for approximately four months.

- When Saturn is retrograde we're held to *personal account*. We can expect situations to arise that force us to ignite and take a stand for our life. We're going over old ground in relation to the reward and recognition that can only come from our applied personal efforts.

- Saturn retrograde is a period in which to practise being diligent, disciplined and patient. Slowly move forward with your tasks and build up a strong foundation beneath yourself. You'll be learning the *art of timing* and building a reputation upon which your life can excel.

Uranus retrograde

Uranus is the third largest known planet in our solar system and is one that has a significant impact on our Earth life. Uranus teaches us to be lively, flexible and anything but boring. Every year it moves in retrograde motion relative to Earth for approximately five months.

- When Uranus is retrograde we feel the need to break free from restriction and cultivate a sense of independence. It's a period for experimenting with enhanced lifestyles and a new, freedom-inducing self-image.

- During Uranus retrograde, you could feel the urge to take more risks and be bold and daring. You'll feel like travelling beyond your norm, so this is a wonderful time of the year for solo or adventure holidays.

Venus retrograde

Venus is the second planet from the Sun in our solar system and is one that is intrinsically (energetically) linked to our heart. Venus moves retrograde approximately once every 18 months and for approximately six weeks at a time.

- When Venus is retrograde it's an empowered period to make over our self-image and the relationship between head and heart, personality and soul. Personal worth and core value become our key themes, as our born-with talents and skills demand to be heard and used.

- During Venus retrograde, you can work on unveiling your authentic inner self. Personal upgrades and clearing your life of any relationships that are out of alignment with who you are, become major priorities.

- It's also the primary cosmic period for working over all personal relationships, as you're more open to being your true self.

Meteor showers

Every year small celestial bodies called meteoroids break into Earth's atmosphere, becoming visible in our night sky as meteors (fireballs, or shooting stars). When meteors occur in clusters we refer to this as a *shower*.

Certain meteor showers happen at the same time of the year, every year. When these showers erupt, I find that they tend to whip up the energy around Earth. They also excite our dream states, increasing the frequency of out-of-body experiences (OBEs) and lucid dreaming. So you may find that your sleep is restless during a meteor shower.

You may also find that you're dreaming of planets and stars, as though you're visiting them and travelling through space *like a star* yourself. Even if you don't physically witness a meteor shower, you can be affected by its energy.

I suggest that you keep a notebook handy as meteor showers occur, because cosmic consciousness will be stirred and your imagination will become flooded with divinely inspired ideas.

CONCLUSION

And so you begin

What a journey we've taken together, through *Cosmic Messengers*. I've felt your presence in every line, guiding my words. Everything I've shared with you has been a lifetime in the making, as it will continue to evolve long after this book is published.

We're works of art, aren't we? Interpreted differently by everyone and multifaceted in what we deliver and express. I so love humanity, and your choice to be here. It's been my honour to write for you and to share a path that I trust you'll find helpful in navigating your reason for being and your cosmic life purpose.

Now that you've read the book, and have begun actively working towards discovering and then realizing your purpose, I suggest that you revisit any chapter that particularly calls to you. Use the valuable reference guides at the end of Parts I and II: they'll help to explain the very real changes that you go through as you upgrade your life and spiral up to the next level of cosmic being.

You can even hold a question in your mind and then intuitively open the book at a random page or chapter that calls to you. When you do this, you'll find the perfect answer and/or a practice that you've been seeking.

The more that you work with *Cosmic Messengers* the deeper your understanding of the universe will grow. This book is here to be a way shower and a guide to help you discover and develop the wisdom of your soul.

Remember that you're an original and that to be totally fulfilled you'll need to prove to yourself, through first-hand experience, what does or doesn't work for you.

It's been my pleasure to open up the energetic cosmos to you, and I trust that you'll fly and flourish, passing on your own inspiring messages as only a Cosmic Messenger can.

I love you. Remember to experience your soul…

Elizabeth x

Notes

Notes

ABOUT THE AUTHOR

Elizabeth Peru

Elizabeth Peru is an internationally recognized Cosmic Guide, spiritual teacher and author. Since 2003, she's been offering her work globally, assisting to uplift and shift humanity with down-to-earth and practical forecasting of upcoming planetary and energy trends.

Elizabeth interacts daily with hundreds of thousands of people across the globe, sharing her knowledge of cosmic energy and the workings of soul and the spiritual dimension. She's passionate about waking people up and bringing cosmic knowledge into the mainstream. Her future energy predictions break down often complex cosmic events into easily understandable, soulful teachings.

Elizabeth's work guides you to access a window into your heart and future, using the cosmic cycles to improve and enhance your life purpose experiences.

Elizabeth welcomes your feedback and interaction about this book and the concepts featured within it. Please reach out and connect with her via her website:

https://www.elizabethperu.com

HAY HOUSE
Look within

Join the conversation about latest products,
events, exclusive offers and more.

f Hay House UK

🐦 @HayHouseUK

📷 @hayhouseuk

💜 healyourlife.com

We'd love to hear from you!